The LITA Guide to No- or Low-Cost Technology Tools for Libraries

Library Information Technology Association (LITA) Guides

Marta Mestrovic Deyrup, Ph.D., Acquisitions Editor
Library Information and Technology Association, a division of the American Library Association

The Library Information Technology Association (LITA) Guides provide information and guidance on topics related to cutting-edge technology for library and IT specialists.

Written by top professionals in the field of technology, the guides are sought after by librarians wishing to learn a new skill or to become current in today's best practices.

Each book in the series has been overseen editorially since conception by LITA and reviewed by LITA members with special expertise in the specialty area of the book.

Established in 1966, LITA is the division of the American Library Association (ALA) that provides its members and the library and information science community as a whole with a forum for discussion, an environment for learning, and a program for actions on the design, development, and implementation of automated and technological systems in the library and information science field.

Approximately twenty-five LITA Guides were published by Neal-Schuman and ALA between 2007 and 2015. Rowman & Littlefield took over publication of the series beginning in late 2015. Books in the series published by Rowman & Littlefield are:

Digitizing Flat Media: Principles and Practices
The Librarian's Introduction to Programming Languages
Library Service Design: A LITA Guide to Holistic Assessment, Insight, and Improvement
Data Visualization: A Guide to Visual Storytelling for Librarians
Mobile Technologies in Libraries: A LITA Guide
Innovative LibGuides Applications
Integrating LibGuides into Library Websites
Protecting Patron Privacy: A LITA Guide
The LITA Leadership Guide: The Librarian as Entrepreneur, Leader, and Technologist
Using Social Media to Build Library Communities: A LITA Guide
Managing Library Technology: A LITA Guide
The LITA Guide to No- or Low-Cost Technology Tools for Libraries

The LITA Guide to No- or Low-Cost Technology Tools for Libraries

Breanne A. Kirsch

ROWMAN & LITTLEFIELD
Lanham • Boulder • New York • London

Published by Rowman & Littlefield
An imprint of The Rowman & Littlefield Publishing Group, Inc.
4501 Forbes Boulevard, Suite 200, Lanham, Maryland 20706
www.rowman.com

Unit A, Whitacre Mews, 26-34 Stannary Street, London SE11 4AB

British Library Cataloguing in Publication Information Available

Library of Congress Cataloging-in-Publication Data Available

ISBN 978-1-5381-0310-4 (cloth : alk. paper) | ISBN 978-1-5381-0311-1 (pbk : alk. paper) | ISBN 978-1-5381-0312-8 (electronic)

♾ ™ The paper used in this publication meets the minimum requirements of American National Standard for Information Sciences Permanence of Paper for Printed Library Materials, ANSI/NISO Z39.48-1992.

Printed in the United States of America

Contents

List of Figures

Preface

Librarians are increasingly being expected to work with a variety of technology tools with little or no training. *The LITA Guide to No- or Low-Cost Technology Tools for Libraries* is an essential text for librarians trying to implement no-cost or low-cost technology tools in their libraries. This LITA guide provides practical ideas and suggestions for discovering technology tools that can be used for a variety of purposes across all library types and more broadly in education. The main parts of this book include technology tools for instruction and teaching as well as outreach and marketing. In addition, there is an appendix on additional educational technologies.

Academic and school librarians will find the chapters on instruction and teaching most helpful, while public and special librarians will be more interested in the chapters on outreach and marketing. All the technology tools discussed have possible applications in all types of libraries. Each reader must consider the purpose of using a technology tool before taking the time to successfully learn how to use the tool and implement it in the library. While librarians could conceivably use all of the tools discussed in this book, it makes more sense to focus on successfully implementing one tool before trying an additional tool.

This book presents the following information, chapter by chapter: the right technology tool depending on its purpose, two technology tools in detail, brief overviews of a few other tools, examples of the tools being used in libraries or education, and a wrap-up of the tools discussed. While there are other books about technology tools or technology in libraries, this is the first book written for librarians and educators with practical information for selecting and implementing affordable and effective technology tools. It is geared toward librarians of all types who are less familiar with technology tools but want to begin using them to improve library services and make their libraries more interactive for patrons and students. Chapters describe how to:

- Create videos with such tools as PowToon and Animaker, which can create animated videos to tell patrons about a new service or teach students about search strategies.
- Produce screencasts with tools like Screencast-O-Matic or Jing, which can demonstrate using a new library database or service.
- Collaborate with such tools as Padlet or Lino, which can be used for student collaboration or teamwork with colleagues and to share project ideas quickly and easily.
- Perform assessment with such tools as Quizizz and Kahoot, which allow for gamified assessment of student or patron knowledge.
- Employ presentation tools, such as Emaze and Academic Presenter, which can create more visually appealing presentations.
- Use marketing tools for social media management, such as Hootsuite or SocialPilot, to save time and make it easy to schedule posts to multiple social media sites.
- Edit and design images with such tools as Canva and Pixlr, which can make image editing easy and more efficient.
- Incorporate digital story creation tools, including Spark and Photo Peach, which can showcase a library service or database.

I have firsthand knowledge of using most of the technology tools highlighted because many of them are used at the University of South Carolina Upstate. Learning how to use the tools in a variety of libraries and educational settings will help you to understand how to use the tools in your own lives. The practical nature of the text will allow you to simply transfer technology tools to your library.

Acknowledgments

I would like to thank my husband, Jonathan Kirsch, for discussing the chapters with me and providing a public library perspective on using the technology tools discussed throughout the book. He was instrumental in my ability to write this book. I would also like to thank Charles Harmon, my Rowman & Littlefield editor. He provided excellent feedback and suggestions of ways to improve the book. Finally, thanks go to the rest of my ILEAD USA team, who helped me create the Find Your Hat website: Lola Bradley, Jonathan Kirsch, Thomas Lide, and Rod Franco.

Introduction

What Are No- or Low-Cost Technology Tools?

Technology pervades every aspect of our lives in the twenty-first century. There are many technology tools that can help librarians and educators improve services and instruction. The phrase *educational technology* has been used for technology tools that can be applied for educational purposes. Many of the technology tools discussed throughout the following chapters could be considered educational technology in their employment in libraries. For example, PowToon or Animaker are technology tools for creating animated videos. In library settings, particularly in school and academic libraries, these animated videos are often used for educational purposes, such as telling students about a new library service, like texting or chatting with a librarian.

Libraries endeavor to share information with patrons and help them become more information literate. Using no- or low-cost technology tools, librarians can inform or educate students and library users. More broadly, many of the tools discussed can also be used to inform or teach a wider audience. Whether at a library conference or while teaching students or discussing the latest James Patterson novel at a book club, librarians can use these technology tools to present and share information.

WHY AND WHEN SHOULD LIBRARIANS USE TECHNOLOGY TOOLS

Some of the following chapters discuss ways and reasons for using specific technology tools, but in general, why should someone read this book? Why use technology tools at all? What are some of the benefits of incorporating no- or low-cost technology tools in libraries? There are several reasons, the number one being context.

Context is important when deciding whether to use a technology tool, so each chapter discusses the purpose of using a tool. It is important to determine the purpose of incorporating a technology tool before jumping in and using it for the first time. Who will be the attendees or target audience, which educational goals are in play, and when will the product be needed? How much time is there to create something, and how long will it take to create? These are all important considerations when deciding on a technology tool to use in a situation.

Each chapter discusses some scenarios and ways librarians can use technology tools, but each librarian must decide if a tool will be helpful in a specific situation. There is no one right answer. Each situation is different, but the chapters also share ways educators and librarians have successfully used the tools to help other librarians decide when it is beneficial to use them in their own contexts.

Some of the general reasons to use technology tools are that they can encourage collaboration and interaction with information and content.[1] No- or low-cost technology tools can also improve efficiency and optimize learning for participants.[2] Depending on the technology tool, they can improve the educational value for participants and engagement with information presented.[3] For example, search strategies are one of the hardest things to teach students because many students believe they are already search experts. Incorporating technology tools can increase student engagement with a lackluster topic in librarianship.

ISSUES TO KEEP IN MIND WHEN DECIDING WHICH TECHNOLOGY TOOL TO CHOOSE

Cost

While most, if not all, of the technology tools discussed in this book are free or have a free version available at the time of writing, there are nonmonetary costs to consider when employing technology tools in the library. One is time. Many librarians wear multiple hats at their libraries and have a wide range of duties that keep them quite busy. This does not allow for a lot of extra time to devote to learning how to use new technology tools. Learning about technology tools does take up some time, but many of the tools in this book are user-friendly and fairly easy to learn. Time is also a factor when using the tools to create videos, edited images, and other products. It can be argued that the time is well spent if the end product is more polished and professional because it will catch library users' or students' attention and be used more than a poorly created product.

While these technology tools have a free version, they may not be free in the future. Technology is constantly changing or updating (just like journal databases). This means that some of the tools discussed in this book will not always be free or may disappear altogether. That is why two tools are highlighted in each chapter and additional tools are also discussed. There will also likely be new tools created that serve the same function. So, while a librarian can become an expert on one technology tool, he or she may need to learn how to use another tool for the same purpose as tools change. This means more time must be devoted to learning the interface for the new tool. Luckily, similar tools usually seem to function in a similar manner even though their interfaces can differ greatly (similar to databases).

One final cost consideration is server or computer space. Most of the chapters focus on technology tools that result in a product of some sort: videos, images, screencasts, and so on. While some of the tools store products on their own servers or websites, it is always best to download (if possible) the product to a library server or computer so the librarians can still use it in case the tool ever disappears. The best practice is to download the end product to at least two locations (computer and external hard drive) so it will be available for future use as needed.

Privacy

Another important consideration with technology tools is privacy. Some tools keep track of all information entered into the tool. For example, the answers and student names for a gamified quiz tool are saved in the system so they can be downloaded by the creator at a later time, but they are also saved in the tool's system for the foreseeable future. While most people may not read the lengthy fine print in the terms and conditions, they often have privacy statements in them that can be helpful to read before using a tool. Educators and librarians looking to enhance ways to safeguard privacy when using no- or low-cost technology tools can also refer to Common Sense Education's guide to protecting data and privacy (https://www.commonsense.org/education/teaching-strategies/protect-your-students-data-and-privacy).

ADA Compliance and Universal Design

A final important consideration when selecting a technology tool is ADA compliance, accessibility, and universal design. Unfortunately, technology tool creators may not be aware of the importance of universal design and being accessible for as many users as possible. Therefore, the librarian should consider this aspect when deciding whether to use a tool. One helpful resource when discovering new tools is a voluntary product accessibility template (VPAT), which provides accessibility information for a tool. Most tools discussed in this book do not have a VPAT available at this point, but accessibility features are being requested from them, and creators are considering adding features more frequently for technology tools.

While VPATs are the easiest to use for determining if a tool is accessible, some tools also have a page or section that discusses accessibility. If the librarian is using the tool to create something to use for the library, then it is less important for the tool itself to be accessible than the end product (unless the librarian is the person who needs the accessibility features). When the tool is being used to create something for the public, then universal design techniques should be incorporated when possible. Universal design is designing something to be accessible to as many people as possible. Margaret King-Sears discusses the seven principles of universal design in learning and technology.[4] Bonnie Fong, Elizabeth Johns, and Becka Rich share some accessibility verifiers to test if screen readers or color contrast work correctly for a website or resource and discuss accessibility and universal design in libraries.[5] These are very helpful for those who aren't as familiar with universal design.

One important thing to remember when creating something like a video or screencast is to always have the information available in multiple formats (use closed captioning when available, and if unavailable in the technology tool, export the video to YouTube if possible and add captions there as well as a transcript). Include alternate text with images online. Some tools may have a text-to-speech feature, such as gamified quiz tools like Quizizz. Librarians should design tools with blind users as well as color-blind users in mind. If red and green are used together in a video scene or image, then they may not be distinguishable for color-blind individuals. Also, some people learn better with different types of media, such as visual, auditory, or text.

Providing items in multiple formats helps to reach the most users or students. It also helps to have a translation available if users speak other languages, like Spanish. It may not be possible to create something that is accessible to 100 percent of the population, but it is important to try to be accessible to as many people as possible. This can be challenging, but as long as universal design techniques are implemented whenever possible, a larger number of patrons will be reached. Cindy Ann Dell, Thomas Dell, and Terry Blackwell provide a final helpful resource of more practical techniques to implement universal design.[6]

NOTES

1. Hossein Zadeh, Arthur Shelley, and Rod McCrohan, "Strategic Considerations for Effective Mapping of Educational Technology to Academic Outcomes," in *Proceedings of the International Conference on Information Management and Evaluation* (January 2011),

461–69,   http://connection.ebscohost.com/c/articles/78120468/strategic-considerations-effective-mapping-educational-technology-academic-outcomes.

2. Lazar Stosic, "The Importance of Educational Technology in Teaching," *International Journal of Cognitive Research in Science, Engineering and Education* 3, no. 1 (2015): 111–14.

3. Ibid.

4. Margaret King-Sears, "Universal Design for Learning: Technology and Pedagogy," *Learning Disability Quarterly* 32, no. 4 (2009): 199–201.

5. Bonnie Fong, Elizabeth M. Johns, and Becka Rich, "Accessibility and Universal Design," *ACRL Instruction Section Tips and Trends*, Winter 2017, http://bit.ly/tipsandtrendswi17.

6. Cindy Ann Dell, Thomas F. Dell, and Terry L. Blackwell, "Applying Universal Design for Learning in Online Courses: Pedagogical and Practical Considerations" *Journal of Educators Online* 23, no. 2 (2015): 166–92, http://files.eric.ed.gov/fulltext/EJ1068401.pdf.

Part I

Instruction and Teaching

Chapter One

Create Videos

Most, if not all, librarians need to create videos for a variety of purposes in their libraries. In academic and school libraries, videos are used primarily for educational purposes. Instructional videos can help improve distance education students' usage of library resources.[1] Animated video creation tools can support learning in creative and original ways, as well as keep students engaged in class content.[2] School librarians can have students create videos to maximize student learning and align with standards, such as Common Core Standards.[3] In public libraries, videos are often used for instructional purposes as well, such as how to use e-book lending services on a variety of platforms. Public libraries may also use videos for marketing purposes. This chapter focuses on the instructional or teaching aspects of video creation, although the tools highlighted could be used for marketing or outreach purposes as well.

When selecting a video creation tool, it is important to think about the main purpose of the video. If the purpose of the video is to introduce a library database, the library catalog, or another library tool, screencasts are a better option for creating a video. For introducing a concept, such as Boolean connectors, LC classification, or plagiarism prevention, an animated video might be a better option to increase engagement. However, if the video is used to introduce the library building or library faculty and staff, then a live-action video might be preferred.

This chapter highlights video animation tools, including PowToon and Animaker. Chapter 2 discusses screencast tools, similar to Camtasia, with free options. Animated videos can be more engaging than a traditional screencast video tutorial. Both types of videos have a place in libraries, and the purpose of the video should be carefully considered before selecting a video creation tool and whether the video should be animated, screencast, or live action.

HOW TO CREATE ANIMATED VIDEOS

The process for creating animated videos can be broken down into a number of steps. For more involved or in-depth videos, it might be helpful to start by creating a storyboard to organize what is to be included in the video. A storyboard is a "sequence of drawings or other images, typically with some directions and dialogue, representing the shots planned for a film, television programme, or advertisement."[4] While it is great if there is a librarian on staff who has the ability to draw excellent storyboards, a basic sketch is also sufficient. The step can be helpful for organizing ideas, but do not spend too much time perfecting a storyboard because this is only the beginning of the process. For shorter videos, there may not be a need for a storyboard. Another alternative to a storyboard is an outline of the purpose or goal of the video, as well as the main content. Similar to an outline for an article, this outline can be the framework for the video.

The next step is to select a video creation tool, whether an animation tool, a screencast tool, or a live-action video with a smartphone or video recording device. When selecting a tool, it is important to think about which tool will best meet the goals or purpose of the video. Once a tool has been chosen, a transcript can be written. It is often a good idea to have a tentative transcript to work from when creating a video. This streamlines the process, especially with longer or more in-depth videos. For shorter videos, it may be fine to begin creating a video without a clear transcript. After a video is created, the transcript can be used to support ADA compliance and to allow for review of the material by patrons. In some contexts, video is not the best mode for relaying information. As an alternative, related handouts or pamphlets can be created from a transcript.

Now it is time to begin creating the video. For an animated video, first choose a theme, background, characters, and objects or props (if necessary or desired). Some animated video tools, such as PowToon, give the option to start with a template. Templates can be helpful for providing ideas of how to use characters or props in interesting ways, particularly if the video creator is a beginner. Once the video creator is more familiar with the tool, videos can be created from scratch.

After the template or theme has been chosen and characters selected, text should be added to the video. This can be accomplished through a voice-over in some tools or with actual text on the screen. Similar to PowerPoint, PowToon and Animaker have slides for each scene that can have different text, characters, or animations. This is when the video elements are put together with text from the outline or transcript. Transitions can also be added between scenes. Once the video elements are added, each scene can be previewed individually or as a whole.

Timing can be the hardest part of creating an animated video. While previewing the video, the timing of characters, props, text, and scenes should be edited. Make sure the viewer has enough time to read the text in a scene before it moves on to the next scene. Additionally, if a character has a thought bubble, make sure there is enough time for the character to arrive, the thought bubble to appear, and the viewer to read the thought bubble before it disappears and the character leaves the scene. It can take a while to set the timing for a longer video. Saving the video is crucial throughout the process because sometimes the Internet goes down or there are other technology glitches. After the timing has been finalized, background music or a voice-over can be added to the video.

Finally, the video should be saved and, if available, uploaded to You-Tube. Once the video is on YouTube, it can be downloaded as an MP4 file and saved in order to have a backup copy. An added benefit of uploading all videos to an individual or library YouTube account is making it easy to embed them in LibGuides or the library's website and share with patrons. After a video has been finalized, the only other step is to periodically check the video to see if it needs to be updated.

PowToon

"PowToon is able to bring concepts alive for students, hold their attention and help them retain information."[5] According to its homepage (https://www.powtoon.com), PowToon animated videos are "proven to be more effective than any other form of video or text communications to grab attention in the workplace." There is a "PowToon for Education" account option for academic and school librarians. The free version of the education account is limited to 100 megabytes of storage and videos up to 5 minutes long. So far, I have created 27 short videos, and there is still room on the free education account. If the storage limit is reached, a classroom basic account can be purchased for $8 per month billed annually (as of 2017).

The regular free version of PowToon also provides 100 megabytes of storage space. The regular pro plan is $19 per month. This means that public librarians may want to choose another animated video creation tool if an abundance of videos will be created. The classroom basic plan is more reasonable at $96 per year. The free version has worked well for the USC Upstate librarians. Each librarian can have their own account, so if one librarian's storage space fills up, another librarian's account can be used to create additional videos. Also, videos can be deleted from the PowToon account, so once the storage is nearly full, videos can be deleted to make room.

One of the advantages about PowToon is that their videos can be exported to YouTube. Although there is no direct download from PowToon with a free account, from YouTube, they can be downloaded to a computer or embedded into LibGuides or other library web pages. This allows for backup of the videos on a library server or an individual librarian's computer. Then the videos could also be used offline for additional situations, such as conference presentations where the Wi-Fi signal may not be reliable.

There are currently two studios in PowToon: HTML5 and Classic Studio. The HTML5 Studio should be used to keep videos more compatible for a variety of devices. The first step in creating a PowToon is to either create a video from scratch, make a storyboard, or begin with a template. Additionally, there is an option to create a square video optimized for social media sites. When first using PowToon, a template may be the easiest way to begin. Once PowToon is more familiar for the librarian, the storyboard feature can be used by selecting a look and then editing the storyboard structure (see figure 1.1). The difference between a template and storyboard is that, with the template, the slides are preselected; with the storyboard, slides must be selected. With either option, all slides can be edited and altered completely from the original slide, giving the video creator the freedom to design every aspect of the video. When the storyboard or template is opened to begin editing, a popup may appear that states "Your PowToon contains PREMIUM (locked) characters and props. If you want to share or download it, please upgrade to our BUSINESS account or delete the object." Then there are options to either upgrade or remove all premium objects. In order to keep the free version, select the "Remove All Premium Objects" option before editing the video.

Once in the editing mode (see figure 1.2), there are many ways to edit the video. Each scene is represented by a different slide on the left side of the page. The scene or slide that is currently selected can be edited by double clicking on one of the text boxes or objects. The timing for text boxes and objects can be edited in the time line at the bottom of the page. On the right side of the page are options to change the layout, background, text, objects, sound, and so on. For example, if "Character" is selected, then different character options are available, such as "Typing," "Happy," "Angry," or "Thinking." At the top of the page are options to name the PowToon; save it; preview it; and export it to Facebook, YouTube, SlideShare, Vimeo, Wistia, or HubSpot. There are also options to download it as a PowerPoint or PDF in the free version.

There are some challenges in using PowToon as an animated video creation tool. PowToon does not have any accessibility or ADA compliance information on the website. There are options for adding captions after a

Figure 1.1. PowToon storyboard example for an explainer video.

PowToon has been uploaded to YouTube, such as the "Automatic Captioning" tool. The automatic captions should definitely be edited because they are often not 100 percent accurate. This is a good option for a PowToon with voice-overs. For text-based PowToons, a transcript should be included with the video. The limitation of five minutes is a challenge, but it can also help the video creator to be succinct and limit the content to one or two concepts rather than trying to include too much material in one video. Another limitation is the number of free objects, characters, and music. There are enough to make a variety of videos, but if more objects are desired, then a premium account must be purchased. Otherwise, there is the option to upload hand-drawn images or photographs in the free version of PowToon. One final challenge is the complexity of the tool. It can be hard to coordinate the timing for different objects and text, but once the tool has been used a few times, this becomes easier.

Animaker

Similar to PowToon, Animaker (https://www.animaker.com) is another animated video creation tool. The limitations with the free version of Animaker are that videos can be two minutes in length, and only five videos can be exported per month. If longer or more videos must be created, then PowToon or another animation video creation tool should be used. The personal plan is currently $9 per month when billed annually or $12 per month when billed monthly. This allows for videos up to 5 minutes each and 20 exports per month.

Animaker begins the video creation process with a variety of templates. For the free version, "Free" should be selected. Then a category can be chosen, such as "Education" or "Infographic" (see figure 1.3). PowToon and Animaker have roughly the same number of templates, but the ability to begin with a storyboard in PowToon makes it more flexible than Animaker.

Figure 1.2.   Layout for creating a PowToon video, including how to add a character to the scene.

There are different characters available in Animaker; many are only available in the premium or paid version. Similar to PowToon, the options on the right side of the page allow for editing the scene with different characters, text boxes, images, music, and so on (see figure 1.4). The different scenes or slides are available on the left side of the page. At the bottom is the time line allowing for manipulation of the length of time objects or text are present in the scene. Finally, the options to save, preview, or export the video are available at the top of the page. Animaker has a very similar layout to PowToon and functions nearly the same, as well. As a result, due to the limitations of Animaker and the additional flexibility in PowToon, PowToon is a better tool to start with when creating animated videos. If many different animated videos are needed, then it may be helpful to use more than one tool to add more diversity in the characters and scenes.

Additional Animated Video Creation Tools

Moovly is a third option for creating animated videos. Moovly allows for an unlimited number of movies up to 10 minutes each. The storage is limited to 100 megabytes or 20 videos. Videos can also be exported to YouTube from Moovly, a great option for longer videos. Rawshorts is another possible animation tool, allowing for only 25 megabytes of storage and uploads to YouTube. One consideration with Rawshorts is that the price is based on the number of exports. For example, three exports cost $60, while ten cost $120.

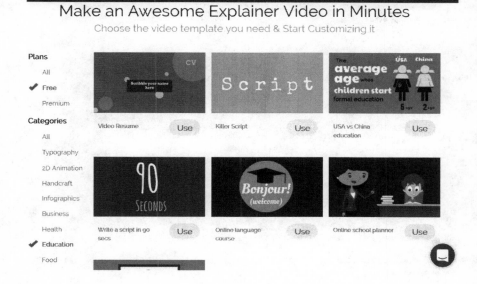

Figure 1.3.   Some examples of Animaker templates for explainer videos.

There are numerous other animated video creation tools, but many do not have a free version. Oftentimes, when a tool becomes more popular, the free version disappears, and only paid versions are available. The librarians at USC Upstate used Xtranormal to create animated videos, but they went out of business; the company that now owns Xtranormal offers only paid accounts. Luckily, the videos were already uploaded to YouTube, so they were not completely lost, but the videos can no longer be edited in Xtranormal. This is one of the reasons it is so important to have a backup of all videos in YouTube or on the library's server.

As far as paid options go, VideoScribe is one of the better-known animated video creation tools. It is a little pricey, at $12 per month when paid annually or a one-off payment of $665. This is a whiteboard animation tool that looks like the creator is drawing a variety of objects and writing text along with a voice-over or music background. These look quite professional when created, but the price is too high for many librarians and libraries.

REAL-WORLD EXAMPLES IN LIBRARIES

At the University of South Carolina Upstate, the librarians regularly create videos to use for instruction, outreach, and course support. Some of the

Figure 1.4.   Layout for creating an Animaker video, including how to add a character to the scene.

librarians teach a three-credit course, Strategies for Information Discovery, often taught online. Animated videos are used to introduce course assignments and what students are expected to do each week for the class (see https://youtu.be/FG9YizbPCFM for an example).

Some of the assignments require students to create videos throughout the class. This promotes technology literacy in addition to information literacy. The New Media Consortium discussed the importance of digital literacy and "empower[ing] students as content and media producers rather than purely knowledge consumers."[6] Animaker and PowToon are introduced to students as possible video creation tools for a technology tools assignment, which they can then use for future class assignments. For example, for the technology tools assignment, in which students test out a video creation tool and share its benefits and drawbacks, one student created a PowToon video about PowToon (https://youtu.be/45Ob9k3mjOk). One educator demonstrates that the highest levels of the revised Bloom's Taxonomy can be achieved when students create original videos for an assignment.[7] She shows a significant increase in student understanding between course lectures and the video creation assignment.[8]

Additionally, animated videos are quick and engaging when explaining such concepts as Boolean connectors to students in one-shot instruction sessions at USC Upstate (see https://youtu.be/k7iokX3yAJw). Other topics lend themselves well to animated videos, like in-text citations (see https://youtu.be/m9ZmOdDaUtk). At the Linebaugh Public Library System, a video was created about the history of the library (https://www.powtoon.com/online-presentation/fEolo8oJHNU/a-brief-history-of-linebaugh-public-library-system/?mode=movie). PowToon was used to create all of these example videos.

School librarian Jennifer Murphy used Animaker to create an outreach video to share with teachers about what the school librarian can do to help students (https://youtu.be/ao7MdrueVpE). Another library used Animaker to remind students about the library's film collection (https://youtu.be/tu4-mW-hRvY).

WRAPPING UP

There are many ways animated videos are helpful for libraries. They can be used to support learning and outreach and to market the library's resources or history. Short, animated videos are a great way to introduce a concept or highlight a library service. Storyboards are good for planning an animated video. PowToon, Animaker, or another animated video creation tool can be used to craft the video. Captions and a transcript should be created for the video to support ADA compliance and possibly create related handouts. A theme, background, characters, objects, text, and music or voice-overs are selected to create a video. Choosing the timing of characters, objects, and text boxes is one of the hardest parts of making an animated video. Whenever possible, it is important to upload the video to YouTube or another video-sharing website and also to download a copy of the video as a backup.

There are benefits and challenges to every technology tool. The video creation tool should be selected carefully in order to best meet the goals of the video. Technology tools can disappear or become paid tools, so it is helpful to become familiar with a variety of animated video creation tools. It is useful to periodically look for new tools to create animated videos because they are always being created. Animated videos are one way libraries can share information with patrons. Such tools as PowToon and Animaker make creating animated videos relatively easy and free.

NOTES

1. Amanda Corbett and Abbie Brown, "The Roles That Librarians and Libraries Play in Distance Education Settings," *Online Journal of Distance Learning Administration* 18, no. 2 (Summer 2015), http://www.westga.edu/%7Edistance/ojdla/summer182/corbett_brown182.html.

2. Nina Sarkar, Wendy Ford, and Christina Manzo, "Engaging Students with Technology in an Asynchronous Learning Environment," *HETS Online Journal* 6, no. 1 (November 2015),

http://hets.org/ejournal/2015/10/29/engaging-students-with-technology-in-an-asynchronous-learning-environment.

3. Kristina A. Holzweiss, "Using Tech Tools for Learning with Standards," *School Library Monthly* 30, no. 4 (January 2014): 13–17.

4. "Storyboard," *OED Online*, September 2016. http://www.oed.com/view/Entry/431843?result=1&rskey=EbWyRm&.

5. Sarkar, Ford, and Manzo, "Engaging Students."

6. B. Alexander, S. Adams Becker, and M. Cummins, *Digital Literacy: An NMC Horizon Project Strategic Brief*, vol. 3.3 (Austin, TX: New Media Consortium, October 2016), 14.

7. Kathryn A. Marley, "Eye on the Gemba: Using Student-Created Videos and the Revised Bloom's Taxonomy to Teach Lean Management," *Journal of Education for Business* 89 (2014): 310–16, https://doi.org/10.1080/08832323.2014.903888.

8. Ibid.

Chapter Two

Produce Screencasts

Screencasts are an important way for librarians to digitally share information with patrons. Chapter 1 discusses the possibilities of creating animated videos for educational and outreach purposes. In some cases, live-action videos are also a good option for marketing or outreach purposes. Screencasts tend to cost less to create and are less labor-intensive than creating a live-action video.[1] Although animated videos can be thoroughly engaging, they are not always the best option for sharing information. Sometimes, the best way to share information is through a screencast.

A screencast tool permits a librarian or educator to "record what is on the screen (PowerPoint presentation, film, drawing, specific software) and captures simultaneously the lecturer's voice commenting and explaining the image."[2] Screencasts are exceptionally suitable for creating videos that demonstrate something, such as how to search a library database or other e-resources. There are a number of benefits of using screencasts in the classroom and for other purposes in libraries. Screencasts allow for more self-directed and enhanced learning; can be paused, replayed, or fast-forwarded; and can be helpful as additional resources to support learning.[3] Morris and Chikwa find that students who viewed screencasts received higher grades than students who did not view them.[4]

Some of the other advantages to screencasts or online tutorials include providing point-of-need instruction, available at all times and from anywhere, and removing some of the restrictions of a one-shot instruction session.[5] Students prefer short, easily accessible, and downloadable screencasts.[6] Allyson Washburn finds that students believe screencasts are effective for delivering information.[7] Learners want to be able to increase the speed at which a screencast is played, prefer screencasts with audio, and want larger screen size and font size.[8] While audio is sometimes troublesome for accessibility, it can make a screencast more interactive and engaging for students. It is helpful to have both a narration of what is occurring on-screen as well as music in the background; both can promote the success of a video.[9] Music for screencasts can be found on a variety of websites, including Free Music Archive, FindSounds, and Freesound.[10] Like when running a library program or teaching a session, it is important to modulate a voice rather than being monotone.

Joanne Oud discusses beneficial guidelines on improving screencast accessibility.[11] Two paid screencast creation tools, Camtasia and Captivate, have the ability to create accessible screencasts, although the "accessibility features must be added through the use of careful planning and proper use of built-in software features."[12] To make a screencast fully accessible, it must provide voice narration and captions that describe the graphics on-screen, control over timing, the ability to pause and replay the video, and text that is size 14 font or larger.[13] YouTube provides some accessibility features with the built-in caption creation feature, but other accessibility options do not work as well in YouTube, so it is important to fully explain what is happening on-screen in the captions as well as the narration. Transcripts can share the information in a video, although captions are preferred. Sometimes, it can be helpful to have both captions and a separate transcript.

To improve usability, make sure visuals have high contrast for easier viewing.[14] Although Oud suggests avoiding background music so it does not interfere with the narration, to make a screencast more engaging, it is important to include background music. Therefore, it is important to test the microphone and how loud music is before recording a screencast. Practicing speaking into the microphone from different distances can improve the narration quality of the screencast and still allow for quiet background music. While cursive or italic text can be visually appealing, it is harder to read; it is better to choose Arial or other sans serif fonts.[15] It can also be helpful to add visual or verbal cues, such as a highlighted box or tone of voice, for the main points in a screencast.[16] Additional things to consider for screencast accessibility include keeping screencasts short and organized with an outline and different sections; being consistent throughout a screencast with fonts, sizes, and colors; avoiding jargon and using simple language and an active voice; and providing instructions if a quiz or clickable area is included in a screencast.[17] Because instructional resources should be available to everyone, it is important to strive for universal design when creating a screencast, and employing accessibility options before creating a screencast can help.

HOW TO CREATE SCREENCASTS

Unlike animated videos, there are a number of articles about creating screencasts and using them for library purposes. Paul Betty includes best practices for creating and managing animated tutorials, including formatting, accessibility, usability, and maintenance best practices.[18] In most cases a screencast should not be longer than five minutes to hold the patron's attention throughout the entire video. If a more in-depth topic must be covered in a screencast, it is helpful to break it up into multiple shorter videos. For example, for a screencast showing how to find and download an e-book to a variety of devices, create a short video for where to find an e-book and individual videos on how to download an e-book onto a MacBook, Windows laptop, iPad, and so on. Breaking up a larger video into segments allows patrons to view the segments they are most interested in rather than forcing them to find the correct spot in a long video. More in-depth screencasts can take up to a month for the entire process, from creating a storyboard to recording and editing the tutorial and posting it on the web.[19] Oftentimes a short screencast can be created in a day, once the librarian becomes familiar with the screencast tool.

Similar to animated videos, screencast creation should begin with a storyboard and transcript for more involved videos. The storyboard can be hand drawn or created in PowerPoint or another storyboard tool. If the best format to meet the purpose of the video is a screencast, then a screencast tool should be selected. There are a number of paid and free screencast tools available. One of the better-known paid tools is TechSmith's Camtasia; another is Adobe Captivate. Some of the free options are Jing by TechSmith and Screencast-O-Matic. These two free tools are discussed in more detail later this chapter.

Once a tool has been selected and a storyboard and transcript prepared, it is time to create the screencast. It is often desirable to include an introduction in a screencast before diving into the demonstration portion of the video, which should be followed by a conclusion or brief recap. It is important to include the library's branding and contact information, either in an introduction or the conclusion to the video.[20] The introduction and conclusion can be created using a PowerPoint slide or two, although some screencast creation tools, including Camtasia, have options for incorporating a title slide that can act as an introduction.

When creating the screencast, it is important to have all of the applications that will be shown during the video open and ready. This includes PowerPoint (for an introduction) if desired; an Internet browser, if showing an online library resource, such as a database; and the screencast tool itself. Once all applications that will be recorded are open and ready, the area for recording should be selected. Usually the size can be altered to accommodate the full monitor screen or part of the screen. If reading from a script, have that ready before starting the recording, try to avoid jargon, and be concise. It is also a good idea to rehearse the recording process and mouse cursor movement, as well as determining how far away the microphone should sit. [21] Next, the recording can begin. Start with the introduction slide (if planning to incorporate); then do a demonstration, followed by a short conclusion. With the free screencast tools, editing is not usually an option. It is easier to learn how to use the free tools because they have less options than the paid tools. The free versions are very basic in nature, and it can take a while to learn all of the editing capabilities with the paid options.

The tool should produce a video that can then be uploaded to the library's website, YouTube, or another video-hosting site. It can be especially helpful to upload the video to YouTube so that captions can be added to the video to make it more accessible. To add captions, go to a YouTube account, and click on "Video Manager." Then select the "Edit" dropdown and click "Subtitles and CC." The video will open up, and then select "English" to see the automatic subtitles (see figure 2.1). Click "Edit" to fix any errors in the captions. Next, click "Publish Edits" to republish them. This process can be viewed on a number of YouTube video tutorials (e.g., https://youtu.be/ukr9v_BIJbE). Although YouTube may update the process for adding and editing captions, there will likely be new videos demonstrating how to incorporate captions into a video. As with animated videos, it is important to download a backup of the screencast from YouTube or other video-hosting site.

After a screencast has been created and edited (when possible), it is important to publicize or market the video so patrons will know about it. Paul Betty discusses some possible ways to market screencasts, including an announcement in the news section of the library website, an article in the student newspaper, bookmarks, and e-mail announcements. [22] For screencasts that are open for all patrons to view, it can be helpful to assess the videos through the use of surveys, Google Analytics, or number of views in YouTube. If a library plans to create a large number of screencasts by a number of different librarians, it can be helpful to create a communications plan for library screencasts. Schumacher and Hendrix have a useful example of how to develop a policy for screencasts in the library. [23]

Screencast-O-Matic

The Screencast-O-Matic tool must be downloaded to a Windows or Mac computer before it can be used (available at http://www.screencast-o-matic.com). Screencast-O-Matic can record the computer screen, a webcam, or both at the same time. This can be helpful if a librarian wants to show themselves speaking as well as the computer screen. Many times, it is easiest

Figure 2.1.   YouTube automatic caption editor view.

to just record the screen. There is a time limit of fifteen minutes in the free version. The area of the screen that will be recorded can be adjusted.

There is an option to pause while recording a screencast to give the time to take a sip of water or change to another application. With the "Pause" hot key, a librarian can begin with an introduction to the library using Power-Point slides and then switch to an Internet browser to show a database, for example. The default is "ALT-P," but it can be changed in the preferences (see figure 2.2).

When the script is ready, press "Rec" to begin recording. There is a three-second countdown before recording begins; start talking after a second or two. Once the recording is complete, click "Pause." The recording can be deleted, if need be, by clicking on the "Recycle Bin" if it was not ready for uploading, or click "Done" if it is ready. Once the video is done, it will appear in a new screen, where it can be previewed, saved as a video file, and uploaded to Screencast-O-Matic or YouTube (see figure 2.3).

The video can be saved as an MP4 (the default), AVI, or FLV. It can be renamed under "Filename." There are also options to highlight the cursor with a yellow circle around it, have just the cursor, or show no cursor. A captions file can also be uploaded here, or captions can be added later in

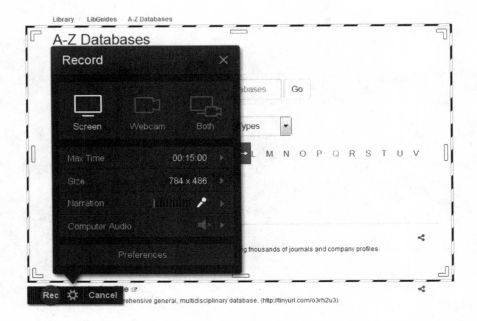

Figure 2.2.   Layout for creating a screencast in Screencast-O-Matic.

YouTube. Choose a folder before clicking "Publish." If uploaded to You-Tube, captions can be added in the video editor.

One downside to Screencast-O-Matic is that the free version does not allow for the capture of computer audio; it just records narration from a microphone. Screencast-O-Matic is easy to use once the basics are learned. It is most helpful for creating quick screencasts to answer a reference question or quickly explain a temporary problem to patrons or students. If a more professional-looking screencast is needed, Jing or one of the paid screencast tools should be used. As with the animation tools, there are benefits and drawbacks to each tool, and a librarian must consider the objectives of a screencast before selecting the best tool.

Jing

Similar to Screencast-O-Matic, Jing should be downloaded (https://www.techsmith.com/download/jing). There are options for Windows and Mac computers. After installing Jing, it should open automatically and produce a small yellow icon in the menu bar and somewhere on the computer desktop. When downloaded on Windows, it appears on the right side of the screen. A microphone should be set up prior to recording a screencast if

Figure 2.3. Screencast-O-Matic options after a screencast is recorded.

narration will be incorporated. Any type of microphone can be used for creating screencasts, although some librarians prefer a headset microphone to avoid moving too near or far from the mic when speaking.

Three options appear when hovering over the icon: "Capture," "History," and "More." "Capture" is used to create a screencast. Next, click and drag the mouse across the area of the screen that will be recorded. Then there is the choice to either take a screenshot or a video recording of the screen. To create a screencast, choose the "Video" option. There is a three-second pause before the recording begins. There are buttons to mute the microphone temporarily, pause, restart, cancel, or stop recording (see the bottom left of figure 2.4). After recording is complete, click the "Stop" button, and the video will open up in a new window. It can then be saved, deleted, or shared via screencast.com. Each Jing video can be up to five minutes long. Narration can be recorded with a microphone. Otherwise, sound playing on the computer can be recorded through the computer's built-in speakers, although the sound quality varies depending on the speakers.

One of the major challenges with Jing is that the video output is saved as an SWF file. YouTube and most other video-hosting sites prefer an MP4 file. There is no direct uploading to video option with Jing. In order to save a Jing video to YouTube, the SWF file must be converted to MP4. There are a

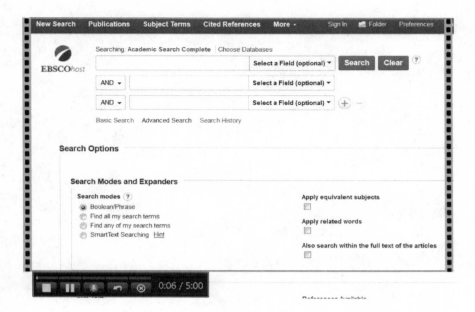

Figure 2.4. View of creating a screencast with Jing.

number of paid and free tools that convert SWF files to MP4 files. It is important to use a tool that is trustworthy. For example, some of the current tools to convert SWF files can be found at http://download.cnet.com/s/swf-converter. A librarian can also search for reviews of a tool before download-ing it to make sure it is legitimate. Of course, it is important to also run an antivirus software. One converter that works as of the writing of this book is Free Flash to MP4 Converter (http://download.cnet.com/Free-Flash-to-MP4-Converter/3000-6676_4-76038288.html).

Additional Screencast Creation Tools

Open Broadcaster Software (https://obsproject.com) is a free, open-source software available to take screencasts. It is a little more complicated to learn than Jing or Screencast-O-Matic, but it does provide another free alternative for creating screencasts. TechSmith's Camtasia and Adobe Captivate are the most popular paid screencast tools. Currently, for an educational, single-user license, it costs $169 for Camtasia and $349 for Captivate (or a subscription for $29.99 per month). Some libraries, particularly academic libraries, can purchase one of the paid screencast tools for librarians to use. For public or school librarians, this is less likely, and the free tools discussed in this chap-ter are more cost-effective. With both Camtasia and Captivate, there are options for adding captions that help make screencasts more accessible, as well as callouts and other features unavailable in the free tools. For those using free screencast software, it is possible to add captions after creating and uploading the video to YouTube.

Guide on the Side (http://code.library.arizona.edu), created by the University of Arizona, is another option for librarians wanting to create interactive tutorials rather than screencasts. Mikkelsen and McMunn-Tetangco looked at Jing videos, Guide on the Side tutorials, student preferences, and how long it took to create an end product with each tool.[24] They found that tutorials took longer to create in Guide on the Side, but they were better for using a flipped-classroom approach to instruction, while Jing videos were better as stand-alone learning objects unconnected to a specific class or assignment.[25] Screencast video tools and tutorial creators both have benefits and challenges. Guide on the Side is a more advanced tool and allows for more interactivity than a screencast; however, it is easier and takes less time to create a screencast. Depending on the purpose of a screencast or tutorial, the librarian must determine the best tool to use.

REAL-WORLD EXAMPLES IN LIBRARIES

At the College of Wooster, Stephen Flynn creates screencasts that are similar to the old choose-your-own-adventure books by giving viewers more choices to allow for more interaction.[26] He created short screencasts and used YouTube annotations as buttons, which linked to the other related screencasts.[27] This allows experienced patrons to skip an introduction, for example, or to choose which segment to watch next in a series of screencasts on a complex topic. It could also be helpful to have students watch a series of screencasts before coming to a library session to save time and allow for more of a workshop rather than a lecture-style class.[28] In order to use this method of making interactive videos, a storyboard between short screencasts should be created, and button graphics must be created in the videos.[29]

The YouTube Video Manager is used to create annotations in YouTube (see https://youtu.be/C5zzVemi3m4 for a tutorial). Keep in mind that YouTube does occasionally change features capabilities. For example, there is no longer an option to pause a video with the "Annotations" feature. Currently, YouTube offers the ability to link to another video, playlist, or approved website. To set up an approved website, the website owner will need to approve a request. This option may be more useful for public libraries, while school and academic libraries may have less control over their websites. Either way, annotations can be used to lead to other library screencasts or animated videos, which allows for more interactivity.

Screencast-O-Matic has been used by public librarians to demonstrate how to use Overdrive to check out e-books (https://youtu.be/SXBcdwqk-hA). Another example is a screencast describing the role of a teacher-librarian in a school library (https://youtu.be/NPS9698g4Ag?list=PLTjeiGlA0 eIqsTScH1n9XZca5-yBiguRt). There are many ways screencasts can be used in all types of libraries, including demonstrating the use of a database or library catalog, downloading e-books, and many others.

WRAPPING UP

There are many uses for videos in libraries. One popular use of videos is to demonstrate a service or resource that the library wants to promote to patrons. An easy way to demonstrate something is through the use of a screencast. Screencast-O-Matic and Jing are two free screencast creation tools. Camtasia and Captivate are the most popular paid screencast tools. Some librarians may only need to create a few short screencasts and prefer creating animated videos, such as those described in chapter 1. In this case, it would be most beneficial to use Screencast-O-Matic to create the screencasts. Some librarians may need to create a large number of screencasts, and so a paid tool might be a better option. As is the case with all of these free technology tools, a librarian must consider the main purpose or goal in creating a video and select a tool that best meets that purpose.

NOTES

1. C. Cox, "From Cameras to Camtasia: Streaming Media without the Stress," *Internet Reference Services Quarterly* 9, nos. 3–4 (2004): 193–200.

2. Cecile Morris and Gladson Chikwa, "Screencasts: How Effective Are They and How Do Students Engage with Them?" *Active Learning in Higher Education* 15, no. 1 (2014): 25–37, https://doi.org/10.1177/1469787413514654.

3. Ibid.

4. Ibid.

5. Allyson Washburn, "Screencasting Library Tutorials for Distance Learners: A User Evaluation." *Indiana Libraries* 28, no. 3: 50, https://journals.iupui.edu/index.php/IndianaLibraries/article/view/19091/18984.

6. Morris and Chikwa. "Screencasts," 25–37.

7. Washburn, "Screencasting Library Tutorials," 52.

8. Ibid., 54.

9. Lucinda Rush and Rachel Stott, "Minute to Learn It: Integrating One-Minute Videos into Information Literacy Programming," *Internet Reference Services Quarterly* 19, nos. 3–4 (2014): 219–32, https://doi.org/10.1080/10875301.2014.978929.

10. Ibid., 226.

11. Joanne Oud, "Improving Screencast Accessibility for People with Disabilities: Guidelines and Techniques," *Internet Reference Services Quarterly* 16, no. 3 (2011): 129–44, https://doi.org/10:1080/10875301.2011.602304.

12. Ibid., 131.

13. Ibid., 129–44.

14. Ibid., 139.

15. Ibid.

16. Ibid.

17. Ibid., 140–41.

18. Paul Betty, "Creation, Management, and Assessment of Library Screencasts: The Regis Libraries Animated Tutorials Project," *Journal of Library Administration* 48, nos. 3–4 (2008): 312–13, https://doi.org/10.1080/01930820802289342.

19. Alyse Ergood, Kristy Padron, and Lauri Rebar, "Making Library Screencast Tutorials: Factors and Processes," *Internet Reference Services Quarterly* 17, no. 2 (2012): 95–107, https://doi.org/10.1080/10875301.2012.725705.

20. Ibid., 100.

21. Ibid., 101.

22. Betty, "Creation, Management, and Assessment," 301.

23. Bridget S. Schumacher and Dean Hendrix, "Developing a Communications Plan for Library Screencasts." *Journal of Library Innovation* 3, no. 2 (2012): 1–17, http://www.libraryinnovation.org/article/view/205.

24. Susan Mikkelsen and Elizabeth McMunn-Tetangco, "Guide on the Side: Testing the Tool and the Tutorials," *Internet Reference Services Quarterly* 19, nos. 3–4 (2014): 271–82, https://doi.org/10.1080/10875301.2014.948252.

25. Ibid., 279.

26. Stephen X. Flynn, "New Adventures in Screencasting," *Public Services Quarterly* 9, no. 2 (2013): 162–68, https://doi.org/10.1080/15228959.2013.785899.

27. Ibid., 163.

28. Ibid., 164.

29. Ibid., 165.

Chapter Three

Collaborate

In all types of libraries, collaboration is important, both among colleagues and among patrons or students. In schools, colleges, and universities, collaboration is important among students in class, and many teachers require group work and assignments. Public libraries often act as community centers and encourage patrons to interact and engage with each other at book clubs and other programs. In other words, collaboration tools are important for all librarians to support patron interactions.

There are a variety of technology tools that encourage collaboration, including social media sites and resource-sharing sites. It is important to consider the purpose of using a collaboration tool before selecting the best tool to use in each situation. For example, marketing library programs or services to patrons may best be accomplished on social media sites, like Facebook or Twitter. When sharing library videos or photographs, it might be best to use a resource sharing site, like Pinterest, YouTube, or Flickr. Many librarians already know how to use social media sites or resource-sharing sites, and there is already a plethora of articles and books related to using these technology tools. Yet for purposes of direct patron or librarian interaction, it is sometimes constructive to use a more private collaboration tool, such as Padlet or Lino, which are discussed in this chapter.

HOW TO USE COLLABORATION TOOLS

To encourage collaboration in a private online setting, a wiki could be used, but this requires login information for each participant, and sometimes these platforms can be less stable because participants can accidently delete content as wiki editors. For more seamless collaboration, a tool like Padlet or

Lino might be more helpful. These act like a virtual corkboard, where anyone with the link to the page can add notes, images, videos, or files.

The first step for using either tool is to set up an individual account or an account for the librarians to share. Then a wall (corkboard) is created and specific format or aesthetic preferences selected. The wall can then be shared with patrons or colleagues for collaboration. Instructions about how to post on a wall may be needed. Then patrons can post pictures, videos, files, or notes to the wall to collaborate and can respond to other's posts.

Padlet

Some may remember Padlet as Wallwisher, its name in 2008 when it was first available. The new name is a combination of the words *paper*, *wood*, and *tablet*.[1] In order to create a wall with Padlet, an account is needed. First, go to https://padlet.com and create an account or use a Google or Facebook account. There are also premium account options that include additional themes, storage, analytics, and privacy, as well as a few other features. Premium account options include the Padlet Jetpack for individuals at $35 per year at the time of publication or Padlet Backpack or Padlet Briefcase for schools or businesses, starting at $12 per month or more for a yearly account based on the number of users.[2] It is wise to begin with a free Padlet account to decide if the tool will be used sufficiently to make it worth purchasing a premium plan. If an individual librarian is using Padlet, it makes the most sense to purchase a Jetpack plan at $35, but for most librarians, the free version is likely adequate. Padlet also has an app for iOS, Android, Kindle, and Chrome, as well as extensions for Firefox, Chrome, WordPress, and Safari.[3]

To create a Padlet, click "New Padlet," select a layout (wall, canvas, stream, grid, or shelf) and a Padlet will be created. Options to modify the wall appear on the right side of the screen. A title can be chosen, as well as a description, wallpaper (background), and posting options, including whether author names are displayed with a post or if comments are allowed on posts (see figure 3.1). Keep in mind that, if someone is not logged in to their Padlet account, their name on posts will be listed as "Anonymous." Unless all participants will have a login, it makes more sense to not include author names with a post and instead request that participants put their names in the title of a post if desired. If the "Modifications" box closes before editing the options, it can be accessed by clicking the cog or gear symbol.

Once modifications have been made, click "Next," and choose the privacy settings: "Private," "Password Protected," "Secret," or "Public." "Secret" often allows for easiest participation but also keeps the wall private from the general public. If "Secret" is selected, then there are options for participants, including "Can Read," "Can Write," "Can Moderate," and "Can Adminis-

Figure 3.1. View of the beginning screen when creating a new Padlet wall.

ter." "Can Read" should be selected when patrons should not be able to add to the wall. "Can Write" should be chosen most often to invite collaboration from participants, so they can add posts but cannot change others' posts or modify the Padlet. "Can Moderate" should be used if another librarian or student assistant will be helping moderate the Padlet. "Can Administer" should not be used unless another librarian co-owns the Padlet and needs full access to it.

Tags can be added if the Padlet is publicly available, and a unique URL ending can be added to make it easier to share with patrons. Additionally, there is an option to uncheck called "Remake," which allows anyone to use a copy of the Padlet as a template for creating their own. Also, moderation requires administration approval before publishing posts, which can be helpful for a librarian to have more control over what is posted, although it adds to the time needed to maintain a Padlet.

Once the settings have been modified as preferred, posts can be created on the Padlet. To create a post, just double-click anywhere on the Padlet, and a box will appear (see figure 3.2). A title can be added to the box, and text can be added to create a note. Otherwise something can be uploaded or attached to a post, including an audio file, a video, an image, a document, or some other type of file. Files can be attached from the web or the computer. Sometimes videos have trouble playing, depending on the program used to create the video or the file type, so it can be beneficial to also include a link to where the video is located.

Padlet is a relatively easy tool to use, which makes it great for collaboration and sharing information, as long as participants have access to the Internet. Sometimes it is unclear to participants how to add a post, so it is often helpful to list instructions for posting in the Padlet description: "To add a

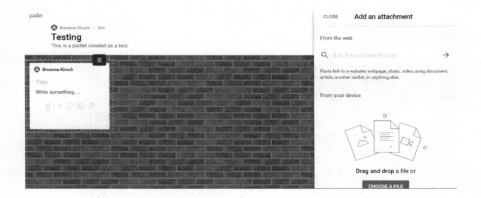

Figure 3.2.   Layout for adding a post within Padlet and adding an attachment.

post, double-click anywhere on the page, and a box will appear." Once a Padlet is completed, it can be shared by using the supplied QR code, available in "Share," the "Share/Export/Embed" tab. It can be saved as an image that can be printed or used on the library's web page or LibGuide when "Print Code" is clicked. Sharing options include copying the link to the Padlet, embedding on a website with an embed code, sending an e-mail, or sharing on Facebook or Twitter. There are also options to export the Padlet: "Save as Image," "Save as PDF," "Save as CSV," "Save as Excel Spreadsheet," or "Print."

There are not many limitations with Padlet. There is a storage limit to the free version, although it has never been reached at the University of South Carolina Upstate's library with the Strategies for Information Discovery course, which regularly uses Padlet for assignment sharing and student feedback and comments. Another minor limitation on the free version is that themes are not available. Themes change the font and color of posts. The posts in the free versions are pretty basic, but because the wallpaper can be changed, it is okay for the posts to be plain. Overall, Padlet is likely helpful for librarians in most circumstances.

Lino

Lino (http://en.linoit.com) is similar to Padlet in its functionality and has been available since 2008. Accounts can be created using a Twitter, Facebook, or Google account or an e-mail address. There are apps for iOS and Android devices. There is also a premium account option with Lino, which includes up to 100 megabytes for an attached file rather than 10 megabytes with the free version. The premium version also allows for unlimited file downloads from Lino, while the free account only allows 10 files to be downloaded per month.[4]

If the purpose is to share attached documents in a shared space, the limitation of 10 files per month makes this tool less helpful than Padlet. For example, it could cause issues for librarians who want patrons to upload a file or document to Lino to share with a group. On the other hand, if the purpose of using the tool is to share ideas and brainstorm or for project management, Lino might be a better option than Padlet because of the "Due Date" feature. There are some additional features in the premium version, but those mentioned here are some of the most important for deciding on which collaboration tool to use.

Once an account has been created, a wall (or "canvas," as Lino refers to it) can be produced. First, click "Create a New Canvas." A new window will open with a spot to name the canvas, background options, and access details. A canvas can be set for private use for only the creator to see; "Show Stickies to Everyone" (others can view but not post); and "Everyone May Post Stickies" (everyone can view and make posts).[5] Additionally, there are options to show the canvas on the dock, create a sticky via e-mail, and generate an RSS for the canvas. These options may be of interest to some librarians, particularly the "RSS Feed" option.

After a canvas has been created, it is time to create posts (or "stickies," as Lino refers to posts). When a canvas opens, there are three boxes that appear on the page, including a "dock," which shows the different canvases for an account, making it easy to switch between them; a calendar; and the sticky toolbox (see figure 3.3). The sticky toolbox provides four different options for sticky color: yellow, green, blue, and pink (traditional sticky note colors). When a sticky is chosen, click and drag it to the canvas. A box with options to be added to the sticky will appear, allowing for tags, changes to the font size (5 options) and color (10 options), the sticky background color (10 options), an icon, a due date, and privacy settings (see figure 3.4). Moreover, there is an option to send the sticky to an e-mail address and a copy can be kept in the canvas.

In the sticky toolbox, there are also options to upload an image, video, document, or clear sticky. Each of these has different options; for example, images have size and type options, while files allow for comments, tags, and font sizes and colors, as well as due dates and privacy. The "Video Upload" asks for a video URL from YouTube or Vimeo and can also be set to private. Each sticky has five options after creation: "Edit," "Set Due Date," "Send This Sticky," "Copy to Another Canvas," and "Peel Off." Most are self-explanatory; "Peel Off" is Lino's method for deleting a post.

Once the different options are understood for Lino, it is fairly easy to use, like Padlet. Some of these options will appeal to school library media specialists or academic librarians who teach students and want to incorporate an

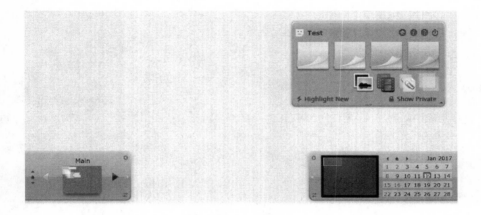

Figure 3.3.   A new Lino page showing the dock, calendar, and sticky toolbox.

assignment into library instruction with a due date. The sticky can also be sent to an e-mail address, allowing for more versatility than Padlet. A canvas could be used to organize a full class as well using different icons for different types of stickies, such as a number for an assignment or a paperclip for a document to read. This might also be useful for librarian colleagues for project management and assigning parts of a project to different librarians with different due dates. This tool allows for options different from Padlet, which might make it better for collaboration among colleagues, while Padlet might be better for student or patron collaboration.

Additional Collaboration Tools

There are a number of other sticky sharing sites or brainstorming pages available. From testing out the different tools, Padlet and Lino are the best options for most library purposes. Scrumblr (http://scrumblr.ca) is one sticky note sharing option. Stormboard (https://www.stormboard.com) is a group brainstorming tool that allows up to five participants, which works for small groups. Spaaze (http://www.spaaze.com/home) and Pinside (http://pinsi.de) are two additional sticky note tools. Richard Byrne reviews each of these tools and compares them to Padlet on his Free Technology for Teachers website.[6] There are a number of other sticky tools, and new ones will come and go. It is helpful for librarians to know about these tools to improve collaboration in an online environment.

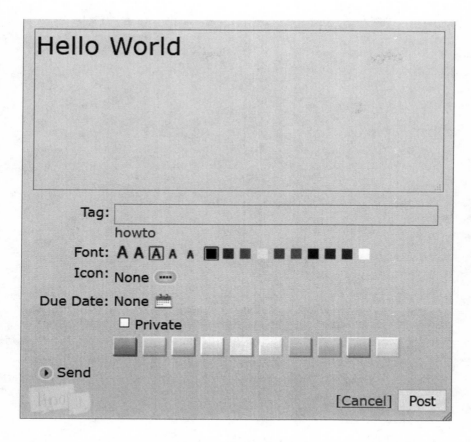

Figure 3.4. Sticky options are displayed, including font size and color, sticky color, and due date.

REAL-WORLD EXAMPLES IN LIBRARIES

Many libraries are making use of Padlet, although it is hard to find examples of libraries using Lino. Many of the same uses of Padlet work in Lino, but Padlet is more popular among librarians. One example of an educator using Lino for his classes is available.[7] He uses Lino and has students participate by posting responses to questions.

Librarian Seth Allen has used Padlet for a variety of purposes, including group activities in instruction sessions, like a resource scavenger hunt.[8] Librarians could also use Padlet like LibGuides; the same type of information can be posted on a wall, although there is more functionality with LibGuides, if a library is able to pay for a subscription. The Unquiet Librarian also has used Padlet for a book tasting to have students participate and share their thoughts on a variety of books.[9] This method allows students to view others' thoughts on a book as they are posted. Macie Hall, an instructional designer, uses Padlet as a virtual exhibition space.[10] Librarian Elaine Patton used Padlet as a brainstorming activity during her library instruction session.[11]

At the University of South Carolina Upstate, librarians have used Padlet for multiple purposes. Padlet walls have been used for Strategies for Information Discovery course assignments, such as a government document assignment (https://padlet.com/bkirsch1/govdocs). A wall was also used to collect resources and slides for a LITA preconference at the 2016 ALA annual conference (https://padlet.com/bkirsch1/preconference).

Richard Byrne discusses the benefits of using collaboration tools, such as Padlet, in education by helping students share more discoveries and research materials than if they worked independently; in addition, Padlet can teach students to defend choices and think critically in evaluating sources.[12] Andy Plemmons is another educator who regularly uses Padlet for collaborative assignments, including those with other schools, such as brainstorming, creating a collaborative thank-you page for a class visitor, collecting ideas and facts for a year-long project, and discussing books and adventures over the summer with students and their families.[13] As these examples show, librarians and educators are using Padlet in a variety of ways, which suggests that this technology tool is beneficial for librarians.

WRAPPING UP

When someone hears *virtual collaboration*, they may think of social media sites like Twitter or Facebook first. Social media sites can be helpful for collaboration in certain situations, but they do not usually meet the needs of working in small groups or allow for much privacy. The tools discussed in this chapter allow for more versatility and sharing options than most social media sites offer. There are many situations in which social media sites are not the best technology tool for collaborating.

Collaboration tools can be used between librarian colleagues or with patrons. Padlet and Lino are just two options that encourage collaboration and sharing of posts. While face-to-face events and collaboration may be preferred, sometimes it is easiest to collaborate virtually on projects, assignments, or programs. While these tools work well for collaborating with others, an individual librarian may want to use Padlet or Lino to collect resources in one space for working on a project or program planning.

NOTES

1. "Padlet: A New Beginning," *Padlet*, 2013, http://blog.padlet.com/2013/02/a-new-beginning.html.

2. "Premium Plans," *Padlet*, accessed January 13, 2017, https://padlet.com/premium.

3. "Apps and Plugins," *Padlet*, accessed January 13, 2017, https://padlet.com/about/apps.

4. "Lino Premium." *Infoteria Corporation*, 2017, http://en.linoit.com/en/premium.

5. *Lino*, http://en.linoit.com.

6. Richard Byrne, "5 Tools for Creating & Sharing Online Corkboards," *Free Technology for Teachers*, February 4, 2015, http://www.freetech4teachers.com/2015/02/5-tools-for-creating-sharing-online.html.

7. Mr. Robertson, "Library Lino It." *Mr. Robertson's Online Classroom*, 2017, http://www.tvdsb.ca/webpages/robertsonj12/index.cfm?subpage=267960.

8. Seth Allen, "Resource Scavenger Hunt," 2017, https://padlet.com/sethallen26/ai1cup1m055i.

9. "Musical Book Tasting + Padlet: A Recipe for Participation," *Unquiet Librarian*, February 19, 2015, https://theunquietlibrarian.wordpress.com/tag/padlet.

10. Macie Hall, "The Virtue of Virtual Exhibitions," *Innovative Instructor*, July 31, 2014, http://ii.library.jhu.edu/tag/padlet.

11. Elaine M. Patton, "Padlet Used for Bibliographic Instruction," *Elaine M. Patton*, August 22, 2013, https://epatton.com/2013/08/22/padlet-used-for-bibliographic-instruction.

12. Richard Byrne, "Collaborative Research Tools," *School Library Journal* 61, no. 3 (2015): 16.

13. Andy Plemmons, "Tech Tutorial Using Padlet to Collaborate beyond Walls." *Library Sparks* 13, no. 5 (2016): 33–35.

Chapter Four

Assess

Many libraries are increasingly pressured to prove their worth in their communities. To demonstrate the importance of libraries, assessments are used to show the usage of library services and materials and how libraries are helping patrons. Public libraries often need to share their usage numbers with trustees or local governments in order to maintain or increase funding. School and academic libraries similarly need to assess student learning to prove that the library and its materials are improving student knowledge and information literacy skills. Quizzes or surveys are given to support library evaluation.

There are many ways to assess library services. This chapter focuses on assessment through quizzes and surveys. Assessment can be helpful for discovering what is missing in a library or what patrons prefer in terms of services and resources. As a patron, it is not usually pleasant to take a quiz or survey. Students in school and academic libraries, in particular, tend to dislike taking quizzes or surveys because they are similar to tests given in their courses. Gamification techniques can make assessment more enjoyable and engaging.

USING GAMIFICATION AS ASSESSMENT

Gamification is defined differently, depending on the context. Karl Kapp provides a definition that works well in education: "gamification is using game-based mechanics, aesthetics and game thinking to engage people, motivate action, promote learning, and solve problems."[1] There are many game mechanics that can be used for gamification. Librarian Carli Spina discusses these as well as benefits and potential problems to incorporating gamification in education.[2] When people think about gamification, points, badges, and leaderboards usually come to mind. These are some aspects of gamification, but gamification has underlying goals to "engage, motivate, promote and solve."[3]

Librarian Bohyun Kim has written a number of articles about how to effectively use gamification in the library. She states, "Gamification used for one-time activity, such as a library orientation or promotional campaign, is not subject to its long-term negative effect on intrinsic motivation. Gamifying an activity that participants find dull or boring is also safe from such concerns because there is little intrinsic motivation to begin with to be undermined by rewards."[4] This suggests that gamification can be helpful for libraries in certain situations, including assessment or feedback.

When looking at how gamification has been used in a variety of educational settings, Dicheva, Dichev, Agre, and Angelova compare the design principles and game mechanics used in a number of articles.[5] They find that social engagement (competition), choice, status (points and leaderboards), freedom to fail, and rapid feedback are the gamification elements used most often in education.[6] The majority of gamification efforts result in higher engagement and increased participation.[7] This suggests that gamification can be used to increase engagement in library events or classes.

HOW TO USE ASSESSMENT TOOLS

While there are many ways to incorporate gamification into library services and programs, this chapter focuses on using gamification in surveys and assessment. Some people may be familiar with using trivia games like *Jeopardy!* in the classroom or library. Teachers and professors sometimes use a *Jeopardy!* PowerPoint to review course materials. This can be fun and engaging for students. Others may be familiar with pub trivia games. These are fun for adults to play, and trivia nights are often well-attended events. There are two gamified assessment tools that allow for *Jeopardy!* or trivia-like experiences.

Generally, to create a gamified assessment or survey, a list of questions and possible answers is needed. Images needed for some or all questions must be ready to use in a folder or on the desktop. These are the only things that must be prepared before creating a survey or quiz in the tools. As far as gamification efforts, creating an assessment is one of the easiest ways to incorporate gamification. The most well-known gamified assessment tool is Kahoot. Another similar tool is Quizizz.

Kahoot

Librarians usually mention Kahoot (https://kahoot.com) when discussing gamified assessment tools at conferences and in articles. Kahoot is a free, game-based learning platform. To create Kahoots and be able to save results, an account must be created. An account type must be selected. As librarians, the option that makes the most sense is usually "Teacher." This works for school media specialists or academic librarians who can list a school or college. Public librarians could select "Business" and list their library name as the organization. Then a user name, e-mail address, and password must be chosen. After an account has been created, it is time to make a Kahoot.

There are four types of Kahoots that can be created: "Quiz," "Jumble," "Discussion," or "Survey." Quizzes are the traditional type of Kahoot for assessment. This is the option used most often by school media specialists and academic librarians. Public librarians will likely want to use the "Survey" option. There may be situations where the "Discussion" or "Jumble" options may be used as well. For example, "Discussion" may be used to quickly ask one question rather than asking multiple questions. A jumble Kahoot can be created when players should place answers in a correct order rather than selecting one correct answer. This could be helpful for training student workers or library pages on call number order for shelving books. A jumble Kahoot could also help librarians or library staff review the order of emergency situation procedures.

When creating a quiz, a title and description must be selected first. A cover image can be added if desired and options set, including to whom the Kahoot is visible (everyone is the default), the language (English is the default), and audience (school, university, business, etc.). There are also options to credit resources and include an introductory video from YouTube. After the options have been selected, it is time to add questions to the quiz.

The question text should be added in the "Question" box; there is a limit of 95 characters for question text. A time limit can be set from 5 seconds to 120 seconds (2 minutes). Points can be awarded in a quiz, and multiple-choice answers should be added (with the limit of 60 characters per answer). Additionally, there are options to add an image or YouTube video for the question (see figure 4.1). Videos can be viewed as a clip or the full video by selecting start and end seconds. There is also an option to credit resources, whether it be the image, YouTube video, or information in the question. The correct answer must be selected by clicking on the check mark next to the answer. Once the question has been created, click "Next." Additional questions can be added until the quiz is complete. Once completed, click "Save" and "I'm done."

After the quiz is completed, it can be played in a classroom or library event or shared with a colleague (if someone else will be running the Kahoot). There are two modes to play a Kahoot: classic (one device per individual) or team mode (multiple individuals share one device and answer questions as a team). Additionally, there are many game options to choose from, such as randomizing the order of questions or answers or using podium,

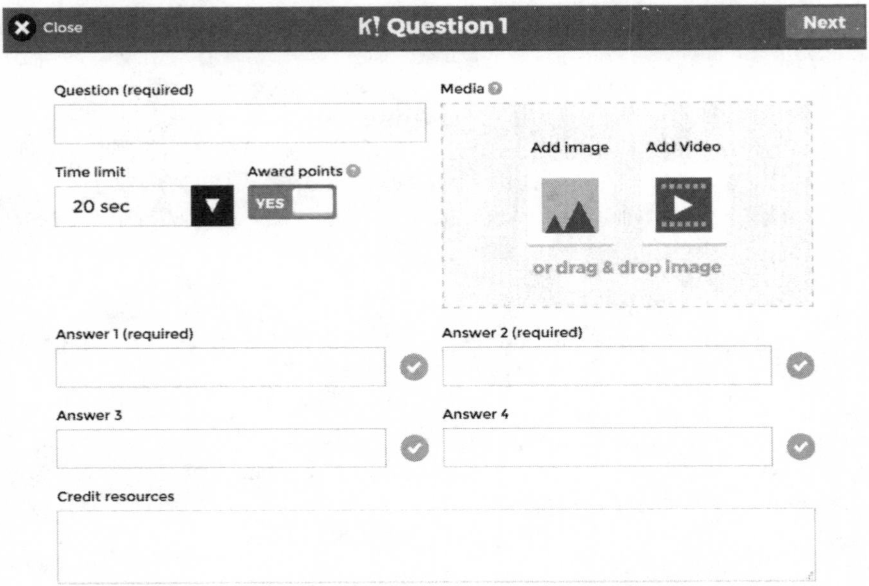

Figure 4.1.   Layout of adding a question in Kahoot and including an image or video.

which celebrates first-, second-, and third-place individuals to increase the level of competition (see figure 4.2).

Now it is time to run the Kahoot. A game PIN will appear at the top of the screen, which is what participants should use to enter the game. They need to open an Internet browser and then go to https://kahoot.it and enter the game PIN before selecting a nickname in order to play. Kahoots work on any device with a web browser and Internet connection and do not require an account or e-mail address to participate. Once all participants are in the game and appear on the screen, click "Start." The first question and possible answers will appear. Participants will see four colors and shapes that correspond to the answers on the librarian's screen (or projector display). They select the answer they think is correct, and then the scores are displayed on the librarian screen. After all of the questions have been answered, the total results will appear and can be saved as an Excel spreadsheet or in Google Drive. This can be extremely helpful for collecting student responses in a one-shot instruction session or class.

A survey or discussion is similar in the steps for creation. Like a quiz, a survey has multiple-choice questions but no correct or incorrect answers, and there are no points assigned or scoreboards, but there will be a bar graph

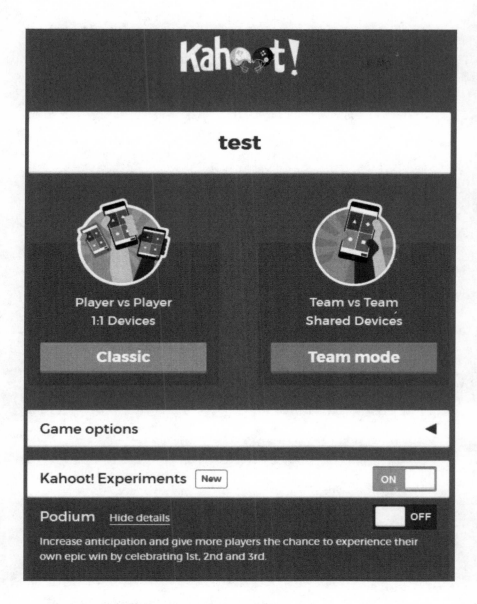

Figure 4.2.   View of the options for playing a Kahoot.

showing how many people selected each answer. All of the game options are
the same for a quiz, discussion, and survey, including the ability for classic or
team modes of play. Jumble is the newest mode for Kahoots. The only
difference with jumble is that answers must be added in the correct order

when creating a question. The order of answers will start out randomized during gameplay. One caveat to a jumble is that the creator may want to say which way to list the order (most to least or least to most, etc.).

Kahoot may seem a little complicated, but it is relatively easy to use once an account has been created and the different types of Kahoots are understood. There are a number of tutorials available on the Kahoot YouTube page (https://www.youtube.com/user/getkahoot/videos). Kahoot is also an accessible tool for most learning disabilities and special needs because of its inclusive design.[8] The Kahoot mobile app has a challenge feature that allows you to assign Kahoots as homework, although students will need to create an account in the Kahoot app in order to participate (see http://bit.ly/2y8shNQ for more details).

Quizizz

Like Kahoot, Quizizz (https://quizizz.com) is another free game-based assessment tool. A live session can be played, just like with Kahoot, but an additional benefit to using Quizizz is the ability to assign a quiz as homework without requiring students to download an app or create an account. Students or patrons can play the quiz outside of the library on their own time. This is extremely helpful for librarians teaching distance-education students, who never meet face to face. While Kahoot is more professional, Quizizz is a great alternative, especially with the homework option. One item to consider is that Quizizz does not allow for a survey option and only allows for questions with one correct answer. This means the tool is not as helpful for librarians trying to gain feedback from patrons regarding a new service or resource.

It is easy to set up a free account with Quizizz by putting in an e-mail address, user name, and password or by signing up with a Google account. Once an account has been created, log in, and then a quiz can be created, or memes can be uploaded to use in quizzes. Memes created for outreach or marketing can be uploaded to Quizizz to use as responses when participants answer questions correctly or incorrectly. If there are no memes to upload, Quizizz has memes that will be used instead.

When it is time to create a quiz, click "Create" and add a quiz image (if desired), a quiz name, and the language, and select if it is public or private. Similar to Kahoot, a multiple-choice question form will appear, and the librarian must fill out the question text and answer options. There is the ability to add an image for the question or insert a symbol. The time for a question ranges from 5 seconds to 15 minutes, allowing for more options than Kahoot in regards to timing.

After a librarian creates multiple quizzes, they can search for questions from other quizzes and add them into a new quiz. There is also an option to make question text different colors: red, green, or blue. Another benefit to Quizizz is that there is no character limit on the length of a question or answers. This is helpful for longer questions and responses. Click "Finish" after the questions and possible answers have been added to the quiz. A grade range and at least one subject must be selected before finishing the quiz. This tool is geared toward teachers, but any grade and subject can be selected even though it may not be accurate. There are also subjects for "Fun," "Professional Development," and "Other," which could be used in most circumstances.

Now the librarian has the option to play the quiz live or assign it as homework (see figure 4.3). Additionally, there is the option to share the administration of the quiz with a link for Twitter, Pinterest, Google Plus, or Facebook. This can be helpful if a librarian is trying to share the quiz with colleagues for them to administer to patrons. When playing the quiz live, there are similar game settings to Kahoot, such as randomizing the order of questions or answers; showing a leaderboard, timer, and memes; and playing music on participant devices. Participants must go to join.quizizz.com and enter a code to join. Then they will enter their name and take the quiz.

When a quiz is run, participants can view the question and answer options on their devices rather than the librarian screen (although they are there as well). This means that, while questions and answers can be as long as a librarian likes, it is best to be succinct and keep them as short as possible to ensure that they are viewable on all devices, including smartphones. Like Kahoot, the results can be exported as an Excel spreadsheet. One nice option with Quizizz is the ability to review questions after the quiz is over, allowing for discussion and examination of the material.

One final feature to discuss for Quizizz is the "Homework" mode. When assigning a quiz as homework, a librarian must set a due date of up to 13 days, 16 hours, and 40 minutes from creating the homework. This means that

Figure 4.3. Layout of Quizizz quiz page.

librarians cannot set a quiz as homework too far in advance (e.g., librarians teaching a semester-long course will not want to set all the quizzes as homework before the start of the course). Other than this constraint, the "Question" and "Game" settings are all the same as a live quiz (see figure 4.4).

Rather than having students complete the game in class, the librarian must distribute the game code and link to participants. There are also student instructions that can easily be copied and pasted to send to participants. The directions are easy to understand:

1. Open https://join.quizizz.com in your browser
2. Enter the 6-digit game code ****** and click "Proceed"
3. Now enter your name and click "Join Game!"
4. You will get an avatar, and then see a "Start Game" button. Click it to begin!

Additional Assessment Tools

There are many assessment tools available to librarians and educators; as far as gamified assessment tools, there are not nearly as many options. Kahoot and Quizizz are best for gamified assessment and feedback. One final assessment tool with a gamified feature is Socrative (https://www.socrative.com). Socrative is a more robust tool than Kahoot or Quizizz, but most of the features do not involve gamification techniques.

Individuals must create an account to participate in Socrative, both as a teacher or as a student. This can be helpful for librarians teaching a full course or who will see participants more regularly throughout the year, such as school media specialists. This tool is not as helpful for public librarians. There are options for quizzes, exit tickets (short surveys to review participants' understanding of material), quick questions (multiple choice, true/false, or short answer), or space race.

The "Space Race" option is the gamified feature that allows individuals or teams to race to complete the quiz first. There is also the option to set up a chat room with a course or groups of up to 150 participants. This allows for different types of usage, but if the goal of the tool is to engage patrons while taking a survey or quiz, then this tool likely is not the best option.

REAL-WORLD EXAMPLES IN LIBRARIES

Richard Byrne discusses how to use Kahoot for a game-based format with quizzes.[9] While Byrne is not a librarian, he writes a monthly column for *School Library Journal*, so his suggestions reach library school media specialists. He was a high school teacher and knows personally how Kahoot works with students. In addition to Byrne's article, there are several other

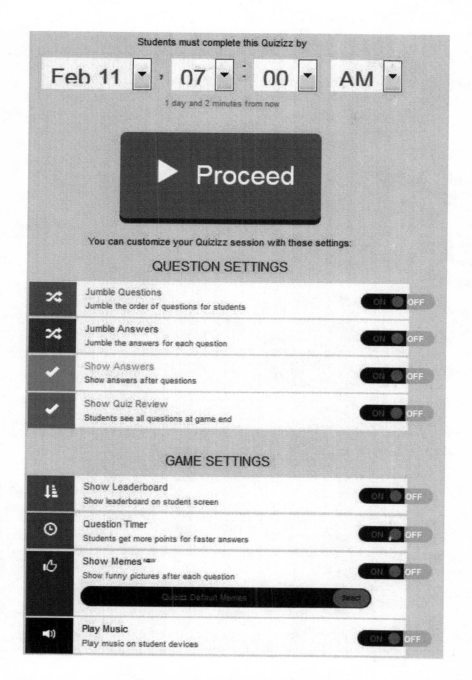

Figure 4.4. "Question" and "Game" settings for assigning a quiz as homework in Quizizz.

library journal articles listing Kahoot as a good tool for librarians, including law librarians [10] and school librarians. [11]

One of the more amusing examples of how Kahoot can be used in libraries is by Lakeview Elementary fourth-graders. [12] Miranda Kral, Solon Community School District librarian, created videos and Kahoots with the help of her fourth graders about credible sources, plagiarism, and book awards to music by Scooter Hayes (Melvil Dewey, international library hip-hop star). [13] Another school librarian, Sara Romine, used Kahoot for her third graders' library orientation. [14]

While Kahoot seems more popular with librarians, there are a number of librarians also using Quizizz, especially school librarians. School librarian Laura Reeb has used Quizizz with her fifth-graders to review and reinforce what they learned in the classroom. [15] Teacher-librarian Lynn Kleinmeyer has collected information about Quizizz as a possible alternative to Kahoot, including video tutorials. [16] Finally, there are examples of library-related quizzes created with Quizizz (https://quizizz.com/profile/55cb88f4e7ca41bf 559e25b2).

At the University of South Carolina Upstate, librarians use Kahoot regularly. In the three-credit Strategies for Information Discovery, Kahoots are used to review course materials once a week if it is a face-to-face course. When the course has been taught online, librarians have instead used the Quizizz homework feature for testing student knowledge on course materials on a weekly basis. They are also used at USC Upstate for flipped one-shot instruction sessions. The professor assigns videos and other materials to students before the library instruction session. Then the librarian gives a Kahoot to test student knowledge of the material and review when necessary before letting students research for their assignments. I have also used Kahoots for conference presentations and at library meetings.

WRAPPING UP

Each librarian must determine if gamification is right for their library patrons and if the benefits outweigh the drawbacks. The two gamified assessment tools discussed in this chapter can engage participants and make a survey or quiz more interactive. Similar to other technology tools, there are benefits and drawbacks, and the decision of which tool to use depends greatly on the circumstances and purpose.

In libraries, there are a number of uses for game-based quizzes or surveys. School and academic librarians can use them to review what students need to know about library resources, search strategies, and other information literacy skills. Public librarians (and other types of librarians) can use these to survey patrons about library preferences or how they feel about a new service. The purpose of using the tool will determine which tool is best for a given situation. For example, Quizizz is best for educational purposes and, specifically, for distance education. Kahoot can be used for various purposes, including evaluation (surveys) and outreach. Despite having fewer gamified options, Socrative might be better for a full-credit course.

NOTES

1. Karl M. Kapp, *The Gamification of Learning and Instruction: Game-Based Methods and Strategies for Training and Education* (San Francisco: Pfeiffer, 2012), 10.

2. Carli Spina, "Gamification in Libraries," in *Games in Libraries: Essays on Using Play to Connect and Instruct*, ed. Breanne A. Kirsch, pp. 62–79 (Jefferson, NC: McFarland, 2014).

3. Ibid., 63.

4. Bohyun Kim, "Designing Gamification in the Right Way," *Library Technology Reports* 51, no. 2 (2015): 33, https://journals.ala.org/index.php/ltr/article/view/5632/6953.

5. Darina Dicheva, Christo Dichev, Gennady Agre, and Galia Angelova, "Gamification in Education: A Systematic Mapping Study," *Journal of Educational Technology & Society* 18, no. 3 (2015): 75–88, http://www.ifets.info/download_pdf.php?j_id=68&a_id=1604.

6. Ibid., 79.

7. Ibid., 83.

8. Johan Brand, "Kahoot!" *Inclusive Design: A People Centered Strategy for Innovation*, accessed February 9, 2017, http://www.inclusivedesign.no/ict/kahoot-article172-261.html.

9. Richard Byrne, "Cool Tools," *School Library Journal* 60, no. 12 (2014): 35.

10. Avery Le, "Technology Essentials: Top 10 Free Computer Tools for Law Librarians," *Computers in Libraries* 35, no. 6 (2015): 10–15, https://search.proquest.com/docview/1701827199?accountid=28698.

11. Pat Miller and Mandy Watson, "Tips from the Trenches," *Library Sparks* 12, no. 3 (2014): 6–7.

12. Miranda Kral, "Melvil Dewey Rocks Library Skills," accessed February 10, 2017, https://www.smore.com/8erav-melvil-dewey-rocks-library-skills.

13. Scooter Hayes, "Store," *Mr. Scooter Storyteller, Kid Hop Artist, and Children's Librarian*, accessed February 10, 2017, https://storyyeller.com/store.

14. Sara Romine, "Technology Tuesday: Kahoot." *Lessons from a Laughing Librarian*, 2014, http://lessonsfromalaughinglibrarian.blogspot.com/2014/08/technology-tuesday-kahoot.html.

15. Laura Reeb, "5th Graders Try Out Quizizz," *Spicewood Library*, 2016, http://spicewoodlibrary.weebly.com/whats-new/5th-graders-try-out-quizizz.

16. Lynn Kleinmeyer, "Quizizz Reference for Using Quizizz in the Classroom," accessed February 10, 2017, https://www.smore.com/kjk58-quizizz.

Part II

Outreach and Marketing

Chapter Five

Present

Many librarians give presentations throughout their careers, whether it's a new project to colleagues, a program for patrons, an instruction session, or at a professional conference. Public speaking can be one of the most challenging tasks, especially for the more introverted librarians. Finding the best presentation tool to make public speaking easier is important. This chapter presents two presentation tools—Emaze and Academic Presenter—that can improve presentations.

There are a multitude of public-speaking resources and courses to improve presentation skills.[1] Sarah Statz wrote an entire book on the topic, *Public Speaking Handbook for Librarians and Information Professionals.*[2] Public-speaking skills can be top notch, but if the slides or presentation tool used are subpar, then attendees will not fully appreciate the presentation. Therefore, it is important to use the best tool for a presentation based on its circumstances. For example, presenting research at a professional library conference requires a different presentation tool than holding an informational program for middle school kids. As stated in the other chapters, it is always important to consider the purpose when determining which tool to use.

HOW TO USE PRESENTATION TOOLS

As many seasoned presenters know, it is important to begin with an outline of what will be discussed. This outline can organize thoughts on a topic and what is important to include in the presentation, as well as act as a starting point for creating slides. Many presenters who incite "death by PowerPoint" include too much text or even all the teaching points on the slides and read directly from them.[3] Relying too heavily on slides can decrease content and presenter interaction for attendees as well as increase passive viewing and tuning out during the presentation.[4]

It is possible to use PowerPoint and avoid these pitfalls, but it is easier to avoid poor presentations with Emaze or Academic Presenter because they lend themselves well toward best practices. Use slides only for complex animation or pictures. Rather than lecturing nonstop, pause and engage attendees between slides so there is time for discourse and questions. Finally, do not distribute handouts of slides because they act as a crutch that interferes with remembering materials.[5] Attendees can take their own notes, which will keep them engaged with the presenter. Slides should facilitate discussion and highlight the main points.[6] Use images that encourage discussion and help retain the content; images are and should be more entertaining than text by itself, which increases audience engagement.[7] Dr. Tresa Kaur Dusaj discusses additional best practices, specifically for PowerPoint slides, although they also transfer well to other presentation tools.[8] She recommends simple slide design, succinct titles and transition slides for different sections of the presentation, clean and readable fonts, concise slide text, and effective graphics.[9] Dusaj also recommends varying the presentation every 10 minutes, such as showing a short YouTube video, administering a short poll, or including a discussion question to make the presentation more interactive and engaging.[10] By incorporating these best practices into presentation slides, a presenter will be the focus rather than the slides. While these methods can be successfully implemented with PowerPoint, Emaze and Academic Presenter can also integrate them into a presentation.

Emaze

A free account can be created at Emaze (https://www.emaze.com), which can be used to design websites, blogs, e-cards, and photo albums in addition to presentations. The "Presentation" option can be used to create an interactive set of slides. One nice feature is the ability to upload PowerPoint slides to create an Emaze, although this feature can have technical glitches. A free account can be upgraded to a premium account for a monthly fee, but the free version is sufficient for most librarians.

It can be helpful to view some of the tutorials available at the Emaze support page (https://Emaze.zendesk.com/hc/en-us). Some of the most helpful tutorials are the "Getting Started Tutorial," "Editor Overview," and "Adding Audio." There are also some helpful FAQs below the tutorials. To create an Emaze presentation, log in and click "Create New" at the top of the "Home" tab. When asked "What do you want to create?" select "Presentation." A series of templates will appear, which are helpful to start with rather than a blank Emaze.

Once a template has been chosen, click "Edit," and it will open the template in the editor mode. The first slide in the template will appear on the screen, and to alter it, highlight text or images. Additional slides can be added by clicking the "Add" button in the top left toolbar (see figure 5.1). To add different parts to the presentation, click "Section." Along the top menu are options to add text, images, media, shapes, or widgets. Widgets for social media accounts can be added, as well as YouTube feeds, a slideshow, or a showcase of images. Keep in mind that social media accounts will need to be connected to Emaze to use this feature. Widgets are also used to add charts. Data can be copied and pasted into the "Charts" widget from a spreadsheet. There are also "Undo" and "Redo" arrow buttons, which can be extremely beneficial when editing an Emaze presentation. Finally, there are buttons for "Copy," "Paste," "Delete," "Save," "Download," "Share," and "View."

The "Download" button works for only premium accounts. There is no option to download the presentation for offline viewing with a free Emaze account, so if the presenter is uncertain of Wi-Fi at a conference, it may be better to use a different presentation tool. When sharing a presentation, there are options to e-mail a link to the presentation, copy a link to share elsewhere, or embed a code on a library's website, LibGuide, Blackboard, or some other location. Additionally, it can be shared to social media accounts, including Facebook, Twitter, Google Plus, LinkedIn, and Pinterest. Finally, the "Collaborate" tab within the "Share" button allows an e-mail recipient to edit the Emaze. It is important to remember that only one person can edit an Emaze at a time. This is a helpful feature for colleagues who work at different libraries but are presenting at a conference together to each edit portions of the Emaze.

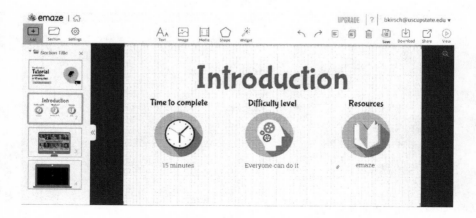

Figure 5.1.   Layout of Emaze dashboard for video editing.

Some major drawbacks to the free version of Emaze are that there is a limit of five presentations and all the presentations are publicly available. There are no options for a private setting in the free version. There are options to only allow a presentation to be viewed or for premium users to download, print, or duplicate the presentation. These can be chosen under the "Share" button in the top menu by clicking the "Privacy" tab and selecting "Public Settings." This might be all right for a conference presentation that will be publicly shared and downloaded or printed. For confidential or private materials, another presentation tool should be used.

When an item is selected on the slide, another menu will appear (see figure 5.2). Depending on the type of item (text box, image, video, etc.), different options are available. Text boxes have options for style, font size, text alignment, bold, text color, background color, effect, opacity, bullets, indents, text direction, hyperlinks, targets, audio, lock, rotate, 3-D, and an advanced menu (which includes line spacing, letter spacing, and font). For an image, the toolbar contains style, color, stroke width and color, effect, opacity, hyperlink, target, audio, arrange, lock, rotate, and 3-D. For a video, the options include editing, style, border width and color, effect, opacity, target, arrange, lock, and 3-D. Opacity allows for different shading of an object; in other words, how faded or transparent it appears. Target allows for different objects in the presentation to be linked for more seamless movement through the presentation. The effect tool allows whichever effect is selected to occur when the mouse hovers over the object. The option for 3-D allows different angles to be altered for a 3-D effect.

One last button is the "Settings" button. This allows for a different theme to be chosen, including color background. The "brand" can be altered as well

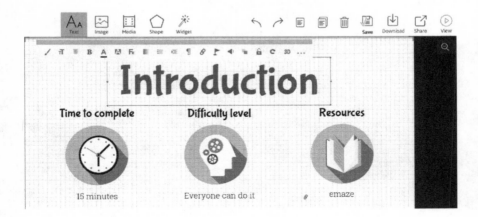

Figure 5.2.   Example of Emaze text editing toolbar.

by selecting different color palettes and fonts, along with table and chart colors. For those who are more tech-savvy, HTML and JavaScript coding can be added in the "Settings" button. Finally, meta tags can be added to visual content to allow more search engines to discover an Emaze presentation if desired.

Overall, Emaze is a fairly user-friendly tool that can make a presentation more engaging. Because Emaze was founded in 2009 and was available in beta mode in May 2013, it is still a new tool that many people do not know about.[11] It was released in the current format in spring 2014. While there are some limitations with the free version, it can compete with PowerPoint and other presentation tools, such as Prezi or Haiku Deck. If a librarian likes how the Emaze presentation looks, then there are also options for creating a website, blog, e-card, or photo album, making this a more versatile tool.

Per the Emaze terms of use, with a free account, a person can store up to five presentations at a time, which means that old Emazes must be deleted once the limit is reached before a new one can be stored. Because of the public settings with the free account, anyone can have a "non-commercial, non-exclusive license to access, view, distribute and publicly display your public Presentations."[12] Because many librarians appreciate open-access initiatives and share their materials with the public or other librarians, this may not be an issue, but it is something to be aware of before creating an Emaze.

Academic Presenter

The Academic Presenter tool is a more complicated presentation tool than Emaze or PowerPoint, but it is also more robust in its capabilities. First, the program must be downloaded to a computer from the Academic Presenter website (https://www.academicpresenter.com/web.faces?page=download). It is in the beta version, so Academic Presenter is still new and will likely be changing over the next few years. It was created by academics from GAK Software (based in Turkey) for academics and is completely free. There is an option to donate to the creators, but all the capabilities are free with the program.[13] Some of the video tutorials are hard to understand because of strong accents and loud background music, but the captions make them easier to follow. Because Academic Presenter is more complicated, the video tutorials (http://bit.ly/2orH66N) are especially important to view before attempting to use the tool. Additionally, there is a free Udemy course on how to use Academic Presenter (https://www.udemy.com/academic-presenter).

The capabilities of this tool make it worth learning even though it is more advanced. Currently, there is only a Windows version. Hopefully there will be a Mac version available in the future. For now, librarians interested in using this tool but who own a Mac will need to run it like a Windows machine or use another presentation tool, such as Emaze or Keynote. Keep in mind that, once a presentation has been created, it can be run on any operating system in the online version.

Once Academic Presenter has been downloaded, it is time to create a presentation. There are templates available (https://www.academic presenter.com/web.faces?page=pap) that can be downloaded and used in the offline version. Templates are probably the easiest way to get started. First, choose and download a template. A video tutorial is available that shows how to open the template in the Academic Presenter program (https://you-tu.be/KS-CS0LxexY). Go to "File," "Open," and choose the downloaded template. This will open the slides as images on the right side of the screen, which can be edited by selecting objects and changing text or images. For example, double-clicking on text will allow editing of the text, color, font, alignment, opacity, and angle (see figure 5.3).

The menu on the left side of the page has tool buttons like those found in Adobe Illustrator or other programs including, "Object Selector," "Free Transform," "Anchor Selector," "Rectangle Marquee," "Filled Rectangle," "Filled Ellipse," "Bezier," "Line," "Image," "Add Movie," "Text," and "Forecolor" (the eyedropper). Most of these buttons allow for an item or shape to be added to the presentation canvas. In the tabs on the right of the screen are "Presentation" (which shows the different slides in the template), "Background" (which allows for editing of the background), "Standard Shapes" (which can be added by double-clicking the shape), and "Final," which changes depending on which type of item is selected, such as text or

Figure 5.3.   Layout of Academic Presenter, including font-editing box.

shape, etc. In this "Final" tab are multiple editing options, including alignment, size, color, and font.

The menu at the top includes "File," "Edit," "Insert," "Run," and "Help." "File" is used to import objects, open a template, save the project, and upload it to a server. "Edit" allows for undo, delete, copy and paste, zoom, replace image, and media manager. "Insert" is where additional objects can be added to the presentation, including the same buttons on the left menu (shapes, image, movie, and text). Additionally, audio, text to speech, latex code (a document preparation system used most frequently for scientific documentation), a PDF, sprites, and handwriting can be inserted (see figure 5.4). "Handwriting" acts as a whiteboard, allowing a presenter to add handwritten notes to the presentation. "Run" is used to show the presentation, and notes can also be made. The "Help" button links to the tutorials, "Donate" page, Facebook, and website. "Help" is also where other languages are available. This changes the words on the page in all the menus to the new language, which can be supportive for international librarians.

Once the layout and tool menus are understood, it is easier to use Academic Presenter. It would be more difficult to create a presentation from scratch, but the tutorials and Udemy course make it doable for most librarians. Because academics created this free tool for other academics, academic librarians may find this tool more helpful than public or school librarians; it tends to be less flashy, but it is completely free and robust in its capabilities. For more tech-savvy librarians, this tool is one to explore.

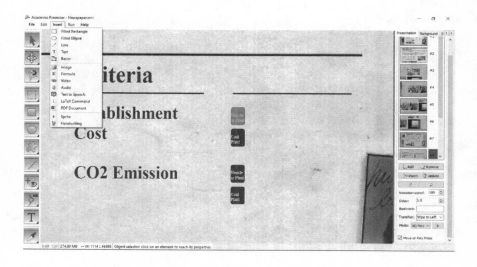

Figure 5.4. Example of what can be inserted into an Academic Presenter presentation.

There are several benefits to using Academic Presenter. Besides Academic Presenter being completely free and more private than Emaze, it also supports a slide layout (like PowerPoint) and a canvas layout (like Prezi) at the same time. This means the presentation can look like a PowerPoint at times and Prezi at others, depending on what the presenter prefers. A presentation can be exported as a PDF file or a PNG image. Additionally, if a PowerPoint presentation is saved as a PNG or JPG file, it can be opened in Academic Presenter. Make sure to select "All Slides" when Microsoft asks which slides to export (see the tutorial for more details at https://youtu.be/ deXsKg2GWSY). Slides must be added to the canvas one by one because they will be saved as multiple images using this method. There is another option to add it as a PDF document, but then each slide will not show up on the screen as an image, and the PDF will need to be clicked to change the slide like a traditional slideshow.

While Emaze is easier to use, Academic Presenter is more robust. As discussed in previous chapters, the best tool for each situation depends on the purpose of the tool as well as the audience and type of privacy needed. For a first-year instruction session or a group of children at school, it might make the most sense to use Emaze if it does not contain confidential materials. For a conference presentation, it might make more sense to use Academic Presenter. Each tool has its benefits and drawbacks. It is best to explore each tool before determining which to use.

Additional Presentation Tools

There are a few other presentation tools available in addition to PowerPoint. One is Sway (https://sway.com), also from Microsoft. It is part of Office 365, for those librarians who have access to it through their library. This tool seems to have less editing capabilities than PowerPoint, but the final product is more aesthetically pleasing. Microsoft describes Sway as a digital storytelling tool that can create interactive reports or presentations.

Many librarians are likely already familiar with Prezi, Keynote, and Haiku Deck. Prezi (https://prezi.com) is a canvas presentation tool that zooms and pans across a large canvas to highlight how different ideas are linked to the overarching presentation topic. It can sometimes be difficult to plan how the Prezi zooms and pans, and it can cause a headache for some viewers. Keynote (http://www.apple.com/keynote) is visually appealing but only available on Mac and iOS devices or PCs with iWork on the iCloud. PowerPoint presentations can be opened and edited in Keynote as well. Haiku Deck (https://www.haikudeck.com) focuses on visuals and uses much less text on slides. This allows for beautiful slideshows, but the free version only permits one publicly shared presentation. This is a major drawback if a librarian plans to give more than one presentation in a short amount of time.

REAL-WORLD EXAMPLES IN LIBRARIES

Because Academic Presenter is still in beta and not many people know about it, there are no publicly available examples of libraries using this tool yet. Because all Emazes are publicly available, however, there many examples of librarians using it. Doing a search for "librarian" under the "Explore" tab of the website brings up more than 100 Emazes created by librarians or about libraries. There is one about virtual reality in the classroom (https://www.Emaze.com/@ATRRQIWQ/virtual-reality-in-the-classroom). Another Emaze is about fake news (https://www.Emaze.com/@ATTLFRWF/all-the-fake-news-thats-fit-to-print). Makerspaces are also featured in Emaze (https://www.Emaze.com/@ALZIQITQ/make-it-and-take). An academic librarian from Rutgers used Emaze to discuss Wikipedia and library instruction (https://www.Emaze.com/@AOTCZQLT/wikipedia-in-library-instruction-lilac). One final example is how a public library introduced e-books and digital services (https://www.Emaze.com/@AOZZLFLQ/pickering-public-library). As is evident in these Emaze examples, some librarians are embracing Emaze as an alternative presentation tool.

WRAPPING UP

This chapter discusses two presentation tools—Emaze and Academic Presenter—as alternatives to the traditional PowerPoint slides. Both tools lend themselves well to creating more engaging presentation visual aids. Public-speaking best practices should be used in conjunction with these tools to allow for a more appealing presentation. While Emaze's free account does not allow for private presentations, it is engaging, visually appealing, and easy to use. Though Academic Presenter is more complicated to use and only available on Windows computers, it has more capabilities than most other presentation tools and is completely free. Because the best tool varies depending on the type of presentation, it is ideal to become familiar with a variety of presentation tools before determining which to use.

NOTES

1. Cathy Belben, "Making a Gift of Yourself: Preparing for Successful Conference Presentations," *Teacher Librarian* 31 (2003), no. 1: 12–14; Cheryl Heser, "Public Speaking 101 for Librarians," *PNLA Quarterly* 76, no. 1 (2011): 70–74; Chapple Langemack, "BOOKTALK Boot Camp," *Public Libraries* 49, no. 1 (2010): 42–51/ Jennifer S. Murray, "10 Steps to Releasing Your Inner Public Speaker: How to Conquer Your Fear and Add to Your Job Skills," *One-Person Library* 23, no. 1 (2006): 7–8; and Eamon C. Tewell, "What Stand-Up Comedians Teach Us about Library Instruction: Four Lessons for the Classroom." *College & Research Libraries News* 75, no. 1 (2014): 28–30.

2. Sarah R. Statz, *Public Speaking Handbook for Librarians and Information Professionals* (Jefferson, NC: McFarland, 2003).

3. John Winn, "Avoiding Death by PowerPoint," *Journal of Professional Issues in Engineering Education and Practice* 129, no. 3 (2003): 115–18, https://doi.org/10.1061/(ASCE)1052-3928(2003)129:3(115).

4. W. R. Klemm, "Computer Slide Shows: A Trap for Bad Teaching," *College Teaching* 55, no. 3 (2010): 122.

5. Ibid., 123–24.

6. Winn, "Avoiding Death by PowerPoint," 116.

7. Ibid., 116–17.

8. Tresa Kaur Dusaj, "Pump Up Your PowerPoint Presentations," *American Nurse Today* 8, no. 7 (2013): 43–46.

9. Ibid., 43–44.

10. Ibid., 44.

11. Barry Levine, "Cloud-Based Presentation Software Emaze (David) Throws $2M at Goliath (aka PowerPoint)," *Venture Beat*, 2014, https://venturebeat.com/2014/11/03/cloud-based-presentation-software-Emaze-david-throws-2m-at-goliath-aka-powerpoint.

12. "Terms of Use," *Emaze*, February 9, 2015, https://www.Emaze.com/terms-of-use.

13. "GAK Software," *LinkedIn*, 2017, https://www.linkedin.com/company/gak-software.

Chapter Six

Market Yourself

It is important to network in all professions, but it can be especially important for librarians to network. Networking can encourage collaborative projects or endeavors across libraries. Online networking with patrons or students is important to market new library services or resources. It does not matter which type of library a librarian works in; social media and online networking is an increasingly important part of librarianship.

There are an ever-expanding number of social media sites to track and update. Facebook and Twitter are the leading social media sites that most people use. For younger patrons and newer librarians, Instagram and YouTube are increasingly important for sharing ideas and content, such as pictures and vlogs. Whichever platforms are used personally or in the library, it is important to regularly update and post so that patrons, students, and fellow librarians continue to follow the account. Keeping up with these various accounts can be a challenge. There are social media management tools that can help. Based on the number of conference programs and articles written about it, Hootsuite seems to be the most popular social media aggregation tool among librarians. There are additional options, though, so it is helpful to compare the tools to see which is best for a librarian or library.

HOW TO USE MARKETING TOOLS

These social media management tools generally work in the same manner. First, an account must be created. Then social media accounts are linked to the management tool by logging into the social media account and giving permission to the tool to access the accounts. Finally, posts can be added to one or multiple social media accounts from within the social media management tool. Usually there is an option to schedule posts in advance for future dates or times. Librarians can also usually respond to mentions or posts related to the library within the social media aggregation tool. These tools tend to be easier to figure out than some of the more in-depth tools discussed in this book. Nonetheless, it is still helpful to see how a tool works and how other librarians are using a tool before attempting to use it in the library.

Hootsuite

To use Hootsuite, go to https://hootsuite.com and create an account. It is important to start with the free account before deciding if it is worth it to upgrade to a paid account. After logging in, click "Add Social Network" to link a social media account to the Hootsuite account. Up to three social media profiles can be added in Hootsuite. At the time of writing, the social media accounts that can be linked to a Hootsuite account are Twitter, Facebook, Google Plus, LinkedIn, WordPress, Instagram, and YouTube. At the University of South Carolina Upstate, the library's Twitter, Facebook, and Instagram accounts are linked to Hootsuite. Permission must be granted to Hootsuite within the social media account. Once an account has been linked, it is time to add streams (see figure 6.1).

Streams in Hootsuite allow for viewing posts or mentions in the social media account within Hootsuite. To add a stream, click "Add Stream" in the

Figure 6.1.   Layout for Hootsuite Twitter streams.

top toolbar. Choose which social media account to add the stream to, and choose a profile (if there are multiple profiles linked to the Hootsuite account). Then the type of stream should be selected. Choices include "Home," "Mentions," "Messages from an Inbox or Outbox," "My Tweets," "Likes," "Retweets," "Scheduled," and "New Followers" for Twitter. In Facebook, options for streams include "Timeline," "Events," and "Scheduled."

The other social media accounts have similar options for streams. Keep in mind that there is also an option to complete a search on the social media site and list the results as a stream. For example, in Twitter, a search for #alaac18 creates a stream with results from Twitter that use the official hashtag for the American Library Association annual conference. Deleting a stream can be accomplished by clicking on the three dots or "Options" button in the top right of the stream and choosing "Delete Stream." Additional options include editing the preferences and displaying text only or text and images.

The toolbar on the left side of the screen provides additional choices in Hootsuite. "Streams," the text bubbles icon, is the default view. The next button is an airplane icon, which leads to the "Publisher" page. This is where posts or tweets can be drafted and scheduled. RSS feeds can also be added and linked to the social networking accounts through Hootsuite. The bar chart represents analytics, and there are some templates or the option to create a custom report. Keep in mind that most of these analytics reports are not available with a free Hootsuite account. The Twitter profile overview report is free and includes information like the number of followers, following, times listed, and follower growth over time. Reports can be shared, downloaded as a PDF, printed, and so on. This can be helpful when presenting marketing data and outreach efforts.

The clipboard icon represents assignments, which can be used if multiple people have access to the account. Campaigns, represented by the ribbon icon, are a newer feature in Hootsuite. These can be used to let followers know about contests, sweepstakes, or galleries. There are more campaign options with paid accounts. The puzzle piece icon leads to the app directory, which allows additional social media sites to be linked within Hootsuite. The final two buttons include "Tools" (education, which leads to tutorials and classes on how to use Hootsuite) and "Help."

Arguably the most important part of Hootsuite is the ability to post to social networking sites from within Hootsuite and to schedule posts in advance. Posts can be scheduled for years in advance, but there is a limit of 30 scheduled posts for free accounts.[1] Messages or posts can be created in the upper part of the page when viewing the Hootsuite streams (see figure 6.2). The profile or profiles to which the messages will be posted should be chosen on the left side of the page. Then the message can be created, and images or links can be attached, as well as a location. Privacy options can also be set here. The calendar icon leads to the scheduling capabilities of Hootsuite if the message will not be posted immediately. A specific date and time can be selected, or the post can be automatically scheduled for "optimal impact." According to Hootsuite, auto-scheduling uses an algorithm that looks at a person's activity and follower's activity through sharing patterns and follower feedback.[2]

SocialPilot

To create a SocialPilot account, go to https://panel.socialpilot.co/login. Then, link the social networking accounts to it by clicking "Accounts" and then "Connect Account" (see figure 6.3). Facebook, Twitter, LinkedIn, Google Plus, Pinterest, Instagram, Tumblr, VK (a Russian-based social networking site), and Xing (similar to LinkedIn) can be linked to SocialPilot. There are two main toolbars in SocialPilot: one in the upper right side of the page and one on the left side of the page. SocialPilot allows 10 posts per day for the free account.

The toolbar on the left side of the page is focused on account options. For example, groups can be created that include a number of social media accounts to differentiate them from other accounts (such as work that includes the library's social media accounts versus personal accounts). "Accounts" is where social media accounts can be connected to SocialPilot or managed. "Posts" is where a post can be created, managed, and scheduled (see figure 6.4). It is also where the URL-shortening tool is located. Unlike Hootsuite, which only allows links to be shortened with Owly, SocialPilot allows a person to use the Google shortener, Bitly, Sniply, and Rebrandly. Shortened links are important for social media purposes because they help the librarian maximize the amount of useful content when posting messages instead of having limited space taken up by long or unwieldy URLs. The "Analytics," "Team and Client," and "Content and Feed" buttons are only for paid accounts. This is one area where Hootsuite is better because it allows for a couple of basic analytics reports in the free version. Finally, there is an "FAQ" button for features that need further explanation.

Figure 6.2.   Hootsuite post and scheduling features.

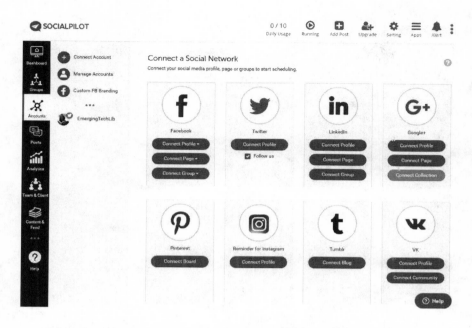

Figure 6.3.   SocialPilot layout and options for linking social network accounts.

The toolbar at the top of the page is where automatic posts can be paused or run. Posts can be added here with the plus sign icon (which leads to the same page as the "Posts" button on the left toolbar). There is a button for upgrading to a paid account, as well as settings for membership, billing (for paid accounts), changing the time zone, URL shortening, and changing the language (English, Spanish, or German are available in beta). The language options are a useful feature with this tool and could be helpful for international librarians or foreign language liaison librarians. The "Apps" button leads to Android and iOS apps as well as extensions for Chrome, Firefox, and Safari, which makes creating posts more seamless. The bell icon, or "Alert" button, opens up the "Notifications" box for things like pausing accounts or enabling sharing. The "Final" button, represented by a drop-down arrow, leads to editing the profile, e-mail settings, changing the password, and logging out.

Overall, the features of SocialPilot and Hootsuite are very similar. Deciding which is better depends on the situation and personal preferences of the librarian. These tools do update periodically, similar to databases and other technology tools. While the interfaces and some functionality may change over time, the basic setup and options will likely remain the same. It might be

Figure 6.4.   The SocialPilot "Create Post" box with scheduling options listed.

best to test-run each tool to see which will work best for the library or personal social media accounts management.

Additional Self-Marketing Tools

There are quite a few social media aggregation tools available, with more created every year. Some also disappear periodically, so it can be advantageous to have a backup tool in mind. Hootsuite is one of the more stable aggregators because it has been popular and available since 2009, but others are becoming more popular. Some of the other available social media management tools include Buffer, TweetDeck, Tweepi, If This Then That, and SocialOomph.

Buffer is one of the more well-known alternatives to Hootsuite. A few librarian articles mention it as a possible tool, though Hootsuite is still preferred in most cases.[3] If This Then That is another tool mentioned in articles referring to Hootsuite alternatives. It uses "applets" to connect different services together; for example, saving Instagram photos to Dropbox. While this tool is not solely a social media management tool, it can be used in this way, although other tools have more functionality specific to social media sites.

TweetDeck has been around for some time as well, but it only aggregates Twitter pages. If Twitter is the only social media account used, then Tweet-Deck is a great tool. Tweepi is another tool that manages only Twitter accounts. The SocialOomph free account only allows for Twitter aggregation, so other tools are likely more beneficial. There are quite a few other tools out there, but most only allow for a free trial rather than a free version with limited capabilities. In the future, some of these tools may stop offering a free account and only offer paid accounts, but because there are multiple tools available with free versions, there will likely be new options for free social media management tools.

REAL-WORLD EXAMPLES IN LIBRARIES

Hootsuite has been discussed at several library conferences and in many articles.[4] At the 2012 annual Virginia Library Association conference, librarians discussed social media and best practices, including using Hootsuite for efficiency.[5] Librarians from the University of South Carolina Upstate have discussed Hootsuite and the benefits of using a social media management tool at multiple conference presentations.

Cybrarian Virginia Mattingly reviewed Hootsuite for the Kentucky Library Association. She discusses that Hootsuite does not require any software installation, so it is available on different computers, tablets, or other devices connected to the Internet.[6] Librarian Ashley Ames Ahlbrand discusses several social media management tools, including Hootsuite, which she uses at her library to keep up with the Twitter and Facebook accounts.[7] Librarian Brandy Klug reviewed Hootsuite and discusses the process of setting up streams and tabs for social media accounts.[8] She also mentions the Hootlet extension for Firefox or Chrome (http://www.hootlet.com), which allows for easy posting of web content to social media accounts.[9] This can make adding web content to social media posts easy and seamless.

Because SocialPilot is a newer tool (first available in July 2014) and less well-known, it is hard to find examples of librarians using it. There are several websites that compare Hootsuite and SocialPilot. One particularly helpful chart from 2016 compares the features of Hootsuite, SocialPilot, and other social media aggregation tools, including Buffer, MavSocial, Social-Oomph, TweetDeck, and Likeable Hub.[10]

WRAPPING UP

Hootsuite and SocialPilot are some of the best tools for managing social media accounts. It can be a daunting task to keep up with posting regularly in the variety of social media platforms that patrons and students use, but social media aggregation tools make this much easier. When selecting an aggregator or management tool, it is important to see which social media platforms can be connected to a tool, and the options and functionality should be explored. Hootsuite is the older and most popular tool, but SocialPilot has very similar capabilities and may appeal more to some librarians. As funds decrease for some libraries, it is more important than ever to market library services and resources, as well as individual librarians. Networking and social media platforms are a frugal way to reach colleagues and patrons.

NOTES

1. "Scheduled Message Update for Free Users," *Hootsuite*, 2017, accessed October 10, 2017, https://help.hootsuite.com/hc/en-us/articles/115009341708.

2. "How Does Auto Scheduler Work?" *Hootsuite*, 2013, accessed April 19, 2017, https://forum.hootsuite.com/discussion/5283763/how-does-auto-scheduler-work.

3. Virginia Mattingly, "Internet Reviews: Hootsuite," *Kentucky Libraries* 75, no. 2 (2011): 14–15; Ashley Ames Ahlbrand, "Tweeted Out: Management Tools to Prevent Social Media from Monopolizing Your Time," *AALL Spectrum* 18, no. 5 (2014): 14–16.

4. North Georgia Associated Libraries, October 14, 2015; Mike Diaz, Clifford Lynch, Karen Downing, and John Dupuis, "Keeping Up with the Things That Matter: Current Awareness Tools and Strategies for Academic Libraries," in *Something's Gotta Give: Charleston Conference Proceedings, 2011*, ed. Beth R. Bernhardt, Leah H. Hinds, and Katina P. Strauch (West Lafayette, IN: Against the Grain Press, 2012), 331.

5. "Virginia Library Association 2012 Annual Conference," *Virginia Libraries* 59, no. 2 (2012): 27–28.

6. Mattingly, "Internet Reviews," 14–15.

7. Ahlbrand, "Tweeted Out," 14–16.

8. Brandy Klug, "Hootsuite Free," *Charleston Advisor* 17, no. 2 (2015): 12–15, https://doi.org/10.5260/chara.17.2.12.

9. Ibid.

10. "Free Social Media Features," *Capterra*, 2016, accessed April 19, 2017, http://blog.capterra.com/wp-content/uploads/2016/03/free-social-media-features-chart.png.

Chapter Seven

Edit and Design Images

A picture is worth 1,000 words—at least that is what the popular idiom states. This is even truer in the current media-focused culture. In order to incorporate images more effectively, it is beneficial for librarians to know about image-editing tools. There are so many ways in which images can be used in professional and personal lives. This chapter is important for most librarians and educators who plan to use images for marketing, educational, or personal purposes.

Visual literacy is important for an increasingly media-rich society.[1] Patrons and librarians alike need visual literacy skills to evaluate and use images appropriately in work and everyday life.[2] Librarian Kristin Henrich discusses the four aspects of visual literacy: finding, manipulating, attributing, and evaluating images.[3] Librarians might teach students or patrons how to find, evaluate, and give attribution to images but are less likely to focus on the image-manipulation part of visual literacy. Some public libraries, on the other hand, may offer classes to the community about image manipulation, which is discussed later in real-world examples in libraries.

Librarians must often edit images to post to library social media sites or to add to a flyer or library newsletter. Images are an important part of any marketing campaign. If a poor image is selected, then it may be harder to catch a patron's interest. With students, patrons, and librarians regularly posting images to Instagram and other sites, it is helpful to know how to edit photos and other images. Because image manipulation is one area that librarians may need more knowledge about, this chapter focuses on image editing and design tools.

Photoshop is the most well-known photo-editing tool. It is also very expensive, making it less cost-effective for many librarians. Luckily, there are a number of free photo- and image-editing tools available. Some tools have been in existence for a while, such as paint.NET and GIMP, which are discussed in a few articles.[4] There are several newer tools that are gaining popularity among librarians, including Canva and Pixlr. Librarians may already know about GIMP or paint.NET because they are older, so this chapter focuses on newer tools that have additional functionalities.

HOW TO USE IMAGE TOOLS

In general, image-manipulation tools usually fall into one (or more) of three categories: web-based, downloadable, or mobile app. Web-based tools can be used entirely online within the tool's website. Downloadable tools require a download, but they can be used offline. Finally, there are an ever-increasing number of mobile apps for smartphones and tablets that are convenient for many library patrons (and librarians). Some tools offer a mobile app in addition to the web-based or downloadable version.

The first step for using an image-editing tool is to go to the website of the tool and either create an account or download the corresponding tool or app. Then an image can be uploaded to edit. Keep in mind that copyright should always be a consideration when manipulating images. Some sites, like Flickr (https://www.flickr.com/creativecommons) or Creative Commons (https:// search.creativecommons.org), allow for image searches to find images that can be modified and can be used for noncommercial uses. There are also sites that share images in the public domain that can be used. Once an image has been selected and opened or uploaded to the image-editing tool, it is time to edit.

There are a number of ways to edit images, but most editing tools allow for cropping an image (cutting out part of the image), adding a filter (to brighten, darken, change color saturation, etc., of the image), and saving the edited image. There are also usually options for the sharing the updated image on social media sites, e-mail, and so on. As mentioned in other chapters, it is important to save an offline copy of the edited image in case the tool ever disappears. It also might be beneficial to try out a couple of tools before deciding which tool will work best for a given circumstance or purpose.

CANVA

Canva is not just an image-editing tool but also a design tool. This is important for librarians responsible for marketing and outreach efforts, particularly those posting to social media sites and wanting to include images. Canva is web-based, first available in 2013, making it one of the newer design and editing tools.[5] The first step is to create a free account, sufficient for most librarians, at https://www.canva.com. If multiple librarians will be creating and editing together, it is helpful to sign up for Canva for Work. Libraries with a 501c(3) nonprofit form or tax-exempt form can create a free Canva for Work account.

Additional options in Canva for Work include collaborating with up to 50 people in the library; an unlimited number of folders to organize designs; a magic resize option for Facebook posts, flyers, posters, and so on; and a brand kit, which keeps consistency across different designs by different people. It is easiest to start with a free account, and if it is deemed to be helpful and necessary, then a Canva for Work account can be created.

After logging in, there are options to look at shared designs and create a team, a design, and your brand. A team can be created with up to 10 members for the free version of Canva. In the "Your Brand" area of the dashboard, one color palette can be chosen. The Canva for Work account allows additional color palettes to be chosen for the brand, as well as default fonts and logos. After exploring the dashboard, it is time to create a design. It is easiest to start with one of the templates provided by Canva. Some of the most popular are shown when first logging in, but more can be viewed by clicking the plug icon. There are templates for social media, presentations, posters, Facebook posts, blog graphics, and more (see figure 7.1).

When a template is selected, a new tab will open in the browser for editing the template into the desired design. The template helps set the correct size for a variety of purposes. Then a layout can be chosen to edit, or personal images or photographs can be uploaded and used (by clicking "Up-

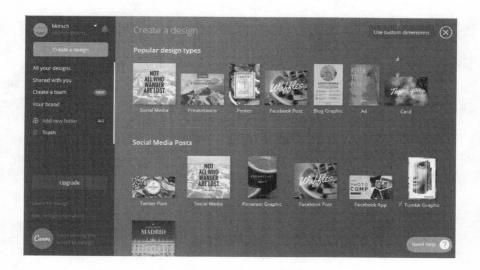

Figure 7.1.   Canva has many design templates to choose from; these are a selection of some of the popular designs and social media post templates.

loads" in the left toolbar and "Upload Your Own Images"). The other tools
on the left side of the page are "Search," "Elements," "Text," and "Background."

"Search" allows the user to see which images are available for a given
search term that can be used in Canva. "Elements" allows the adding of free
photos, grids, frames, shapes, lines, illustrations, icons, charts, and Canva
graphics (see figure 7.2). This can create a better design quickly and effi-
ciently. "Text" can be used to add a heading, subheading, body text, or a
variety of font and text styles. "Background" adds basic colors as a background or an assortment of textured colors. Keep in mind that all of these
tools (besides the "Uploads" button) have free and premium options. Be sure
to only select the free options; otherwise, premium items must be paid for
before the graphic can be downloaded for use.

After an item has been added to the Canva template, it can be edited with
a variety of options in an upper toolbar. For example, clicking on a text item
allows the user to change the font, size, color, alignment, bold, italics, list, or
spacing. Additional options listed under "More" include "Arrange" (send the
item forward or back), "Transparency (make the item more or less see-
through), and "Link" (to external websites). Other elements, including
shapes, lines, illustrations, icons, and charts, consist of basic editing options,
such as basic color changes, copy, arrange, transparency, and link. Double-
clicking an added chart allows for the label and values to be edited, in
addition to the colors, style, size, and so on. When the value is changed, the
corresponding value changes on the chart (or graph). Charts are one of the
newer features of Canva.

**Figure 7.2.   The Canva editing view shows examples of the types of elements
that can be added to the creation.**

A free photo used under the "Elements" tool can be edited. Clicking on a photo allows the user to filter it with premade filters or adjust the brightness and contrast. Advanced options for filtering include saturation (how brilliant the colors are), tint (adding a color tint to the image), blur (how sharp or blurry the image is), x-process (making the image have a higher contrast and less natural colors), and vignette (making the periphery less bright to emphasize the center). Additionally, photos can be cropped, flipped, or copied. Similar to the text boxes, arrange, transparency, and link can also be edited.

Overall, Canva is an intuitive tool to use. Its capabilities far outweigh other image-editing tools because there are more design options, making this tool more like Adobe InDesign than Adobe Photoshop. It can seem a little complicated at first, especially with the free options mixed in with the premium (paid) options, but once a librarian becomes familiar with looking for the free options, Canva is a helpful design and editing tool. If a librarian needs to design a flyer or add text to an image, Canva is likely the best tool. If photo editing is the primary need, then another tool might be better, such as Pixlr.

Pixlr

Pixlr (https://pixlr.com) is entirely a photo-editing tool. One of the benefits of Pixlr is that no account is needed to be able to edit a photograph. Pixlr is another web-based tool, and there are three different Pixlr editing tools: Pixlr Editor, Pixlr Express, and Pixlr-o-matic. Pixlr Express and Pixlr-o-matic are basic editing tools, while Pixlr Editor is more comprehensive and similar to the functionality of Photoshop. Express may be the most helpful option for Instagram photos because it includes red-eye correction; teeth whitener; and hundreds of filters, artistic overlays, borders, and text layers as well as a collage maker. For social media images, Pixlr Express can be particularly useful. Pixlr-o-matic is even more basic and only includes the filters, borders, and overlay options. It does offer more options than Instagram, so it could be better for librarians who are editing photos primarily within Instagram.

If a librarian is interested in a more robust photo-editing tool, Pixlr Editor is the free tool to use. There are editing options, including layers, filters, and color and correction tools. Because Editor is more comprehensive, this is the version discussed in this chapter, although the other Pixlr versions are worth exploring as well. When Pixlr Editor is opened, there are the following options: "Create a New Image," "Open Image from Computer," "Open Image from URL," or "Open Image from Library" (in Pixlr, Facebook, or another library). Using the "Library" option requires a Pixlr account. It is likely easiest to start with an image from the computer or a URL (although copyright must be considered when deciding to use someone else's image).

At first, Pixlr Editor can seem complicated, but once the options are understood, this tool is easy to use. Perhaps the easiest section to understand is the menu across the top of the page. The menu includes "File," "Edit," "Image," "Layer," "Adjustment," "Filter," "View," "Language," "Help," "Font," "Login," and "Sign Up" (see figure 7.3). "File" and "Edit" are very similar to other programs in functionality. "Image" edits the size and rotation of the image and canvas (editable area). "Layer" adds another layer to work with and edit. "Adjustment" offers more well-known editing options, such as brightness and contrast, hue and saturation, or color vibrancy and balance. "Filter" offers similar filters that can be found in other photo-editing platforms like Instagram. "View" provides zoom options and viewing different boxes that can be closed, like "Navigator," "Layers," or "History." One nice feature in Pixlr is the amount of languages to choose from under the language menu. This can be helpful when working with international students or patrons. The "Help" menu leads to "FAQs," "Help," "Pixlr Blog," and "Contact Information." The newest menu item is "Font," which contains "Free Fonts," "Premium Fonts," "Font Bundles," and "How to use your own fonts." These link to https://thehungryjped.com/fonts. Canva is easier to use for different fonts, so if a librarian needs to use multiple fonts, it will likely be simpler to use Canva.

The tools on the left side of the page are similar to Adobe Illustrator and other editing tools. There is a lasso tool, wand tool, pencil, brush, eraser, paint bucket, gradient, clone stamp, color replace tool, drawing tool, and more (see figure 7.4). Some tools overlap with the options in the menus, so it is important to explore the various tools and menu items before using Pixlr

Figure 7.3.   The Pixlr Editor has menus with multiple tools and options. This image shows the items under each menu.

Editor. There are also boxes for "Navigator," "Layers," and "History" (of editing the image).

Because Pixlr Editor has many options, it can be helpful to view a video tutorial or two before using the tool for the first time. A useful beginner's tutorial available on YouTube is from LifeThroughAndreasEyes (https://you-tu.be/eH0VVWHKCIs). Searching for "Pixlr tutorial" in YouTube brings up a variety of helpful videos on the various tools in Pixlr and how they work. Pixlr has capabilities similar to Adobe Photoshop and Illustrator, making it helpful to know about and refer patrons to when they need a photo-editing tool. Parts of it can be a little complicated to learn if unfamiliar with photo-editing tools, but the tutorials can easily help a person learn how to use Pixlr. When a robust editing tool is needed, Pixlr is a helpful one to use.

Additional Image-Editing Tools

There have been several web-based photo-editing tools in the past that were bought by other companies or no longer exist. There will likely be additional photo-editing tools in the future, particularly for smartphone and tablet applications. FotoFlexer (http://fotoflexer.com) is another web-based image-editing tool. This tool seems to have less functionality than Pixlr Editor, but it does seem simpler to use if a person is just beginning to use a photo- or image-editing tool.

Paint.NET is a well-known image editor because it is like Microsoft Paint (present on all PCs), but it has more capabilities. It was released in 2004 and has had a number of updates since then.[6] Paint.NET must be downloaded to a Windows PC from https://www.getpaint.net. GIMP (GNU Image Manipula-

Figure 7.4. The "Adjustment" menu for a photo provides editing capabilities similar to Photoshop and other photo-editing tools.

tion Program; https://www.gimp.org) is another photo-editing tool that needs to be downloaded in order to use it. GIMP was first released in the 1990s and has been updated multiple times.[7] While both tools are free, GIMP is open source and available for Linux and OSX, in addition to Windows PCs. Both of these tools work well for editing images, but some libraries do not allow programs to be downloaded onto work computers. This makes web-based tools more accessible for use by most librarians.

REAL-WORLD EXAMPLES IN LIBRARIES

In addition to librarians needing to edit images for their own work and everyday lives, they sometimes also help students or patrons learn how to use photo-editing software or tools. A number of public libraries have offered programs teaching patrons how to use Pixlr Editor.[8] Both public and academic libraries list Pixlr as a helpful photo-editing tool, often comparing it to Photoshop.[9] Some librarians have blogged about the benefits of using Pixlr for editing images.[10] Librarian Brian White at the Poplar White Station Public Library shares handouts for his Pixlr program that can also be helpful for librarians new to Pixlr.[11]

Canva similarly has been reviewed by several librarians on blogs.[12] Librarian Ashley Chasse has made her Canva designs available at https://www.canva.com/ashleychasse. Other librarians use Canva to create flyers, reports and infographics, signage, and digital graphics.[13] At the University of South Carolina Upstate, librarian Virginia Cononie uses Canva regularly for outreach and marketing efforts. It is often used to create social media posts and flyers to highlight library resources and services (see https://uscupstate.libguides.com/OnlineInstructionalResources).

WRAPPING UP

Pixlr and Canva are just two of the available image-editing tools, but they both are web-based and freely available to use. Because they have some overlap but focus on different aspects, it is helpful to learn how to use both tools simultaneously before choosing one for regular use. Canva is a better option for designing marketing and outreach materials, while Pixlr is better for editing photos. Depending on what a librarian is trying to create or edit, each tool is beneficial to know. Both are valuable alternatives for paid photo-editing tools, like Photoshop.

NOTES

1. Kristin J. Henrich, "Visual Literacy for Librarians: Learning Skills and Promoting Best Practices," *Idaho Librarian* 64, no. 1 (Spring 2014): 16, https://theidaholibrarian.wordpress.com.

2. Ibid.

3. Ibid.

4. Ibid.; Donna Block, "No Photoshop? No Problem! Digital Photography Programs on a Budget." *Young Adult Library Services* 9, no. 2 (Winter 2011): 16–18, http://www.ala.org/yalsa/young-adult-library-services; Steve Hargadon, "The Best of the Web—for Shutterbugs," *School Library Journal* 55, no. 4 (April 2009): 17, http://www.slj.com.

5. Sarah Perez, "Backed by $3 Million in Funding, Canva Launches a Graphic Design Platform Anyone Can Use," *TechCrunch*, August 26, 2013, https://techcrunch.com/2013/08/26/backed-by-3-million-in-funding-canva-launches-a-graphic-design-platform-anyone-can-use.

6. "Roadmap and Change Log," *paint.NET*, accessed May 4, 2017, https://www.getpaint.net/roadmap.html.

7. "GIMP History," *GIMP*, accessed May 4, 2017, https://www.gimp.org/about/history.html.

8. *Chicago Ridge Public Library*, http://chicagoridgelibrary.org/events/photo-editing-with-pixlr-editor; *Elmwood Park Public Library*, http://www.elmwoodparklibrary.org/about-eppl/newsletters/enewsletter-archive/listid-1/mailid-110-library-update-nov-16?tmpl=component; *New York Public Library*, https://www.nypl.org/events/programs/2017/05/24/photo-editing-beginners-using-pixlr; *Princeton Public Library*, https://www.princetonlibrary.org/event/photo-editing-paint-pixlr-editor.

9. *Benedictine University*, http://researchguides.ben.edu/c.php?g=201871&p=2591322#s-lg-box-7925090; *Calvert Library*, http://calvert.lib.md.us/software.html; *Town of Ulster Public Library*, http://townofulsterlibrary.org; *University of Michigan School of Information*, http://makerbridge.si.umich.edu/2013/02/pixlr; *University of Victoria*, https://www.uvic.ca/systems/support/web/contentmanagement/resizeimage.php.

10. Dana DeFebbo, "A Bit of Bytes—Photo Editors," *Informed Librarian Online*, 2013, http://www.informedlibrarian.com/BitofBytes.cfm?FILE=bb1307.html&PrinterFriendly=Y; Brian White, "Pixlr Fundamentals: Handouts," *Librarian Rolodex*, http://librarianrolodex.blogspot.com/p/pixlr-fundamentals-handouts.html.

11. White, "Pixlr Fundamentals."

12. Ashley Chasse, "Another Canva Addict," *Ashley Chasse Blog*, http://ashleychasse.com/another-canva-addict; Jess, "Canva for Work—Free for Libraries!" *5 Min Librarian* April 8, 2016, http://www.5minlib.com/2016/04/canva-for-work-free-for-libraries.html.

13. Brooke Ahrens, "Technology Tuesday—4 Ways to Use Canva in Your Library," *Knowledge Quest Blog*, December 16, 2014, http://knowledgequest.aasl.org/technology-tuesday-4-ways-use-canva-library.

Chapter Eight

Digital Storytelling

Once library photographs have been edited using Pixlr or Canva (see chapter 7 for more details), it is time to share the images. Images are effective for sharing information about the library and services, but creating a digital story can be even more effective. What is a digital story? The basic definition involves telling a story with computer-based tools.[1] A digital story is similar to a narrated slideshow except with more options to incorporate text, video, images, music, and narration. Digital stories make use of multiple forms of media to share a story.[2] There are several reasons librarians might use digital stories to share information with students or patrons.

Using digital stories in libraries is discussed in detail in several educational and instructional books.[3] Kristen Rebmann, library science professor at San Jose State University, discusses some of the reasons librarians might use digital stories, including highlighting voices and public libraries as knowledge centers, while academic and school libraries can have students create digital stories that reach a variety of learning styles (visual, kinesthetic, and auditory) and promote twenty-first-century literacies.[4] Kelly Czarnecki is the technology education librarian at the Charlotte Mecklenburg Library, and she writes about how digital stories can help foster interpersonal skills, interactive communication, personal and social responsibility, technology literacy, curiosity and creativity, and basic and visual literacy.[5] Public libraries, in particular, may use digital stories to tell their own story, although there are certainly applications in academic and school libraries, as well, beyond educational purposes. Digital stories are one possible avenue for telling the library's story to patrons. This chapter focuses on the digital storytelling tools Spark and Photo Peach.

HOW TO USE DIGITAL STORY TOOLS

Before using a digital story creation tool, it is important to plan the story using digital story elements. The 10 elements considered by students at the University of Houston are the purpose of the story, narrator's point of view, questions to answer, content, clarity of voice, narrative pacing, audio soundtrack and multimedia elements, story detail, and grammar and language usage.[6] After considering these elements, it is time to work through the steps of creating a digital story.

Educators Sara Kajder, Glen Bull, and Susan Albaugh discuss a seven-step process for creating digital stories:

1. Write an initial script.
2. Plan an accompanying storyboard.
3. Discuss and revise the script.
4. Sequence the images in the video editor.
5. Add the narrative track.
6. Add special effects and transitions.
7. Add a musical soundtrack.[7]

Not all of these steps must be used every single time a digital story is created, but it is helpful to think about whether each element and step should be included depending on the purpose for creating a digital story. For example, for shorter digital stories, it may make the most sense to skip the storyboard step and move directly to putting the images in order. It is helpful to consider the different parts of the creation process to make sure the resulting digital story meets the goals and purpose of the story.

Another important consideration when creating digital stories is copyright. Many librarians may already realize the importance of copyright and using only images, video, and audio created by the library or digital story creator, in the public domain, or in the Creative Commons. Students will likely need extra help with this, and pointing them toward helpful resources for finding images and audio in the Creative Commons is an important phase in the process of teaching digital stories. Stony Brook University has a helpful LibGuide on copyright-friendly resources.[8]

Now it is time to create a digital story. Follow the steps for creating a digital story: Write a script, and put together a storyboard (as needed). Pick out images and video or music to add to the digital story. Then put them in order and add narration to the images, either through text on the image or an audio narration. Finally add music, special effects, and transitions. These are fairly straightforward steps, and the digital storytelling tools make it seamless.

Once the digital story has been created, it is important to preview the story and ask colleagues to view the digital story before sharing it with patrons or students. Check the timing, grammar, and typos. Once the digital story is ready, it is time to share it. Different tools have different ways of sharing a digital story. Some allow for the creator to download the story and share it offline. Others provide a link to share the story. Some also offer the option to embed digital stories on websites or social media pages. The librarian must determine the best way to share the digital story (within the capabilities of the digital story creation tool).

Spark

Spark (https://spark.adobe.com) is a free web-based graphic design tool that can be used to create digital stories as well as animated videos and graphics. An account can be created with Facebook, a Google account, an Adobe ID, or an e-mail address. Once an account has been created, it is time to create a digital story. This can be accomplished by clicking the red plus sign under "Video." To begin, it might be easiest to use a template to create a digital story.

For example, choose "Teach a Lesson." First, a title must be chosen, although this can be changed later in the editing process. A quick, one-minute tutorial appears before the editing screen. It is helpful to view this tutorial because it orients the creator to the editing features in Spark. Once the tutorial has been viewed, the editing screen will be available, complete with writing prompts of what could be included on each slide (see figure 8.1).

The editing screen is similar to PowerPoint; there are slides and options for each slide with the layout and what to include. Each slide can contain a video, photo, or icon and text. Additionally, the microphone can be used to create a voice-over for each slide. The options are simple and intuitive, and Spark is one of the easiest tools for creating a digital story. The layout options for the slides are on the right side of the page: "Fullscreen," "Split Screen," "Caption," and "Title and Text." Test each of the layouts before choosing one for the first slide so it is easier to decide how to arrange the story.

When adding a photo, one can be uploaded or found in a search, the creative cloud, Lightroom (another Adobe product), Dropbox, or Google photos. The search looks for images related to a keyword on Google, Flickr, and others with Creative Commons filters. It is always important to double-check the Creative Commons license terms and follow those to avoid copyright infringement. The safest method is to only use images created by the librarian or library colleagues, but adding Creative Commons images can

Figure 8.1.   The editing layout for Spark provides writing prompts for what can be included on each slide.

also add variety and professionalism to a digital story. One can similarly search for icons in the Creative Commons for use in the project.

Choosing to add a video will open a box to browse the computer for a video. Only videos already saved on your computer can be imported and used in Spark. There is a maximum of 30 seconds of video allowed on a slide, which means the video is segmented to a 30-second time frame. This timeframe can be edited by sliding or dragging the ends of the video clip. Additional parts of the video can be added on other slides as well if more than 30 seconds of the video will be used in the digital story. Finally, choosing to add text is a simple function that adds a text box on the slide.

Besides the layouts, there are two other options in the upper right of the editing screen: "Themes" and "Music." "Themes" allows a creator to choose a different background with different colors and change the font and colors of the text. "Music" allows a creator to add their own music or choose one of the freely available options in Spark, such as soundtracks that are happy, playful, relaxed, and so on. Don't forget to add narration to each slide (if desired) by using the microphone icon in the middle of each slide. The first time the microphone is selected, it will ask to use the computer's microphone. Once access has been allowed, the microphone icon should be pushed and held using the computer mouse while speaking. Once the narration is completed, let up on the mouse, and it can be previewed by clicking the play button on the left side of the slide. If a narration needs to be re-recorded, just click and hold down on the microphone again.

Once a digital story is completed to the creator's satisfaction, click "Preview" at the top middle of the screen to view the completed project. After reviewing the video and making any necessary edits, it is time to share the story by clicking "Share" at the top of the page (see figure 8.2). This is when the title for the digital story can be changed. A category must be selected. Usually the "Education," "Events," or "Stories" categories make the most sense for librarians. A subtitle can also be included, and the author's name can be visible or hidden by clicking the "On and Off" slider button.

More options allow for editing the photo credits and adding personal credits. One of the helpful features of Spark is that the Creative Commons images and icons will automatically add photo credits for the creator into this section, making it easy to cite sources used in the digital story. With the free version, there is Spark branding. In order to remove this branding, an Adobe Creative Cloud account must be purchased. Also, there is the option to remove the video from possibly being featured on the Spark website. Finally, there is the ability to either download the video as an MP4 or create a link to the video. Creating a shareable link allows for sharing with Facebook, Twit-

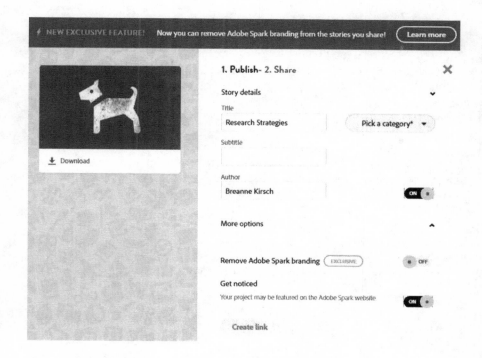

Figure 8.2. Options for Spark story titles are available in the "Share Story" window.

ter, and e-mail or getting an embed code. The video is hosted on the Spark website. Similar to the previous chapters, it is best to download the video and save it on a library device so that, if Spark ever disappears or the free version goes away, the video can still be used.

Some helpful resources are available from Adobe including the inspiration gallery (https://spark.adobe.com/gallery) and blog (https://spark.adobe.com/blog). Both resources can encourage ideas and provide a starting point for projects and possibilities. This can also be a useful resource for helping community members or older students to think about ideas for creating a digital story for a program or class assignment. In addition to the web-based version of Spark, there are apps available for iOS devices, including Spark Post, Spark Page, and Spark Video. Spark Video is likely the best app for creating digital stories, although Spark Page also has some applications for digital stories.

Overall, Spark is arguably the easiest and most professional of the free digital story creation tools. There are other tools that work just as well, but the usability of Spark makes it my preferred digital story creation tool. There are still some challenges with Spark. Adding text into a video does not allow for many editing capabilities—the font, color, and size change automatically based on the theme, layout, and amount of text. This cannot be edited, although it is designed to be aesthetically pleasing and is likely sufficient for most cases. Where the font and color of the text is important, it can always be added to an image or colored background and saved and uploaded as a photo. Another challenge is that the video clips are limited to 30 seconds at a time, although as mentioned previously, a video can be split over multiple slides if longer videos need to be included.

Photo Peach

Photo Peach (https://photopeach.com) is another digital storytelling tool. To create a free account, click "Sign Up for Free" or "Sign In with Facebook" to use a Facebook account. Once an account has been created, log in. Keep in mind that Flash Player is needed to use this tool, so it is less mobile device–friendly. For some librarians, Spark is the better tool to use. For school librarians or academic librarians teaching in a computer lab, Photo Peach might be a good option.

Photo Peach has a free account, but they also have a premium account and a class premium account option for educators. At the time of writing, the individual premium account costs $3 per month, and the class premium account varies from $9 per month for 50 students to $25 a month for 150 students. More details about the differences between the free and premium accounts can be found at https://photopeach.com/education/premium. For most librarians, the free account is sufficient. Limitations to the free version of Photo Peach include the limit of 30 photos per digital story, no option to upload music, and inability to be downloaded. Even with these limitations, Photo Peach is a good option because there are fewer editing capabilities, making it easier to learn and quicker for creating digital stories, particularly for librarians teaching patrons or students how to create a quick and easy digital story.

Now it is time to create a digital story using Photo Peach. After logging in, click "Upload Photos" and link where it shows "Create New Slideshow." Choose up to 30 photos to include in the digital story. There is not a size limitation for the photographs or format limitations (as long as it is an image file). If a librarian wants to include more than 30 photographs, a collage can be created (with a tool like Collage Maker; https://www.befunky.com/features/collage-maker) and used as one image. Photos already saved on the computer are the only images that can be added to Photo Peach. This diminishes the risk of copyright infringement. If other people's images must be included, they can be saved onto the computer before uploading to Photo Peach. Introducing digital storytelling to students or patrons is a good moment to teach copyright and fair use. If 30 large photos are chosen, it may take a little while for them all to upload to Photo Peach. Once they all upload, the photos can be rearranged like a storyboard, which is helpful for visually organizing the story.

After reordering, click "Next," and choose a slideshow title, description, and background music (from the music options available within Photo Peach or from a YouTube video that will play during the slideshow). The speed can also be changed for the amount of time spent on each image in the digital story, although the default is usually a good speed for viewing ease of the audience. Keep in mind that the description is what is used for creating the captions on each image, so it can be helpful to have the captions already written before finishing the digital story. They can also be edited after finishing the video. At this point, the video can be shared through Facebook, MySpace, Twitter, e-mail, or an embed code in a blog or downloaded (the download option is only available with a premium account). If the digital story must be edited, click on the wrench "Edit" button on the upper right of the video.

Figure 8.3 shows the editing screen in Photo Peach. The options at the top of the page allow for changing the settings for the video ("Public," "Unlisted," or "Invitation Required"); editing captions, photos, music, and title; adding photos; managing comments; deleting the show; and downloading the show (again, only available with premium accounts). The option likely to be most useful is editing captions and photos. Each slide or image can be edited individually by clicking on the text for the caption and editing as needed. There are also options for creating a blank slide, copying a slide, or deleting a slide on the right side of the screen. The speed can be edited on the bottom of the slide and previewed. To stop the preview, just click the "Preview" button again.

Possibly the most interesting feature of Photo Peach is the customizable caption on the left side of the slide. "Center" and "Bottom" move the caption to the center of the slide or the bottom of the slide. The quiz option allows for incorporating a short quiz question into the digital story (see figure 8.4). This is a great option for school or academic librarians who want to use a digital story to introduce a topic to students, such as search strategies. Screenshots of databases could be used, and then a quiz question about Boolean connectors could be incorporated directly into the digital story. When viewing the digital story, students would select an answer and discover immediately if they chose the correct answer. There is not a way to see which answer

Figure 8.3.   This Photo Peach editing screen shows what a quiz question looks like for a viewer.

students selected, but this can be a valuable learning tool that is more interactive than just viewing a basic digital story. The quiz option allows for a short question and three multiple-choice answers.

While the quiz functionality makes Photo Peach an interesting option for creating a digital story, there are definitely some drawbacks to this tool. There are no customization options with Photo Peach other than those listed here. Font, size, and color cannot be changed. There is a limit to the amount of text that can be added to a slide. There is no option to add narration to the slide like there is in Spark. The functionality and capabilities of Photo Peach are drastically reduced when compared with Spark. This could be good for certain circumstances; for example, when teaching students how to create a basic digital story. One final drawback is that photos cannot be rotated in Photo Peach. Landscape and portrait-oriented photos can both be used, but if they are saved sideways, they will be shown sideways, and there is no way to change it at this time. Be sure that photos are rotated and saved correctly before uploading them to Photo Peach. As long as the challenges are consid-

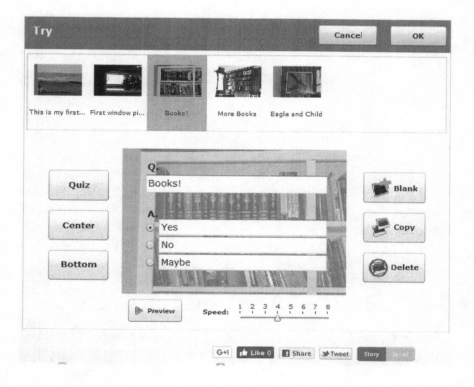

Figure 8.4.   When editing a slide in Photo Peach, a quiz question can be added, and the speed and location of the question can be changed.

ered ahead of time and these drawbacks are not a concern, Photo Peach can be a useful tool, particularly its quiz feature. In the majority of situations, Spark is a better tool.

Additional Digital Storytelling Tools

As with other educational technology tools, there are additional options for digital storytelling tools. Probably the most widely known digital story creating tools are iMovie and Windows Movie Maker. They are device-specific and less user-friendly than the web-based tools discussed in this chapter. For librarians wanting to create and not teach others about creating digital stories, iMovie or Windows Movie Maker are good tools. For librarians wanting to teach others how to create digital stories, it might be better to introduce a web-based tool that can be used on a variety of platforms.

Capzles is another web-based tool that some educators are successfully using in their classes. Capzles is similar to Photo Peach, although in some ways it is more difficult to use. Images, videos, MP3s, Word, Excel, Power-Point, and PDFs can be uploaded, which allows for more functionality than either Spark or Photo Peach, but the tool is less user-friendly and uses Adobe Flash. There are also options to change the font, size, and color of text. Although there are more editing capabilities in Capzles, it is less seamless and projects are set up more like a time line, with all photos displayed in a row at once, rather than set up like a video, as in Spark and Photo Peach. Choosing a tool depends on a librarian's preference, as well as the tool's purpose.

REAL-WORLD EXAMPLES IN LIBRARIES

There are a number of librarians who have used both Spark and Photo Peach individually and in the classroom. The Primrose Hill Library Media Center had students create digital stories about creation myths using Photo Peach (available http://phlib.weebly.com/porquoi.html). Another school librarian had her fifth-grade class create book trailers with Photo Peach (https://www.coetail.com/gemlibrary/tag/photopeach). Toledo Library has also used Photo Peach to highlight the library building (https://photopeach.com/album/byaakw).

Jennifer Hanson, director of Library Services at Worcester Academy in Massachusetts, reviews Spark and discusses how easy to use it is.[9] Librarian Emily Zorea uses Spark to create flyers for her library.[10] Educator Richard Byrne likewise reviews Spark for educational purposes.[11] School librarian Maya Bery has her students create book trailers with Spark.[12] The University of North Carolina at Charlotte holds workshops for students on how to use Spark.[13] Spark is still a fairly new tool, only available since 2016, so as more librarians hear about it, it will likely become a more popular tool for creating digital stories (and for other uses).

WRAPPING UP

This chapter introduces two tools for creating digital stories. They can be used to promote library services or the library itself. They can also be used to teach students and patrons about how to create their own digital stories. Spark and Photo Peach can both create a beautiful digital story, but they have different capabilities that a librarian must consider depending on the circumstances.

Spark and Photo Peach both have strengths and weaknesses. Spark has more functionality, and the results tend to look more professional than other digital story tools. Photo Peach has limited functionality, but this can be good depending on what a librarian wants to do with the tool. Photo Peach also has the option of adding quiz questions throughout the story, making this a particularly helpful tool for school and academic librarians. No matter which tool is used, it is important to remember the elements and process of creating a digital story.

NOTES

1. Bernard Robin, "About Digital Storytelling," *The Educational Uses of Digital Storytelling Website, University of Houston College of Education*, accessed June 11, 2016, http://digitalstorytelling.coe.uh.edu.

2. Rebecca J. Morris, "Creating, Viewing, and Assessing: Fluid Roles of the Student Self in Digital Storytelling," *School Libraries Worldwide* 29, no. 2 (2013): 54–68.

3. Kelly Czarnecki, *Digital Storytelling in Practice*, Library Technology Reports 45, no. 7 (Chicago: ALATechSource, 2009); Anne M. Fields and Karen R. Diaz, *Fostering Community through Digital Storytelling* (Westport, CT: Libraries Unlimited, 2008); and Patricia McGee, *The Instructional Value of Digital Storytelling: Higher Education, Professional, & Adult Learning Settings* (New York: Routledge, 2014).

4. Kristen R. Rebmann, "Theory, Practice, Tools: Catching Up with Digital Storytelling," *Teacher Librarian* 39, no. 3 (2012): 30–34.

5. Czarnecki, *Digital Storytelling*."

6. Robin, "About Digital Storytelling."

7. Sara Kajder, Glen Bull, and Susan Albaugh, "Constructing Digital Stories," *Learning & Leading with Technology* 32, no. 5 (2005): 40–42.

8. Darren Chase, "Copyright Friendly Resources," *Stony Brook University Libraries*, last modified June 2, 2017, http://guides.library.stonybrook.edu/copyrightfriendly.

9. Jennifer Hanson, "Web Stories and Social Graphics Made Easy with Adobe Spark," *School Library Journal Review*, last modified August 2, 2016, http://www.slj.com/2016/08/reviews/tech/web-stories-and-social-graphics-made-easy-with-adobe-spark-slj-review.

10. Emily Zorea, "Things That Changed My (Library) Life in 2016," *Sowing Seeds Librarian*, last modified January 11, 2017, https://sowingseedslibrarian.com/2017/01/11/things-that-changed-my-library-life-in-2016/#more-391.

11. Richard Byrne, "10 Ways to Use Adobe Spark in School," *Free Technology for Teachers*, last modified May 25, 2016, http://www.freetech4teachers.com/2016/05/10-ways-to-use-adobe-spark-in-school.html#.WT3yzsa1u00.

12. Maya Bery, "Book Trailers with Adobe Spark Video," *Maya Bery Weebly Blog*, last modified February 14, 2017, http://mayabery.weebly.com/blog/book-trailers-with-adobe-spark.

13. J. Murrey Atkins Library, "Adobe Spark: Add a 'Spark' to Your Visual Presentations," *UNC Charlotte LibGuides*, last modified May 10, 2017. https://library.uncc.edu/event/974.

Appendix

Where to Find Educational Technology Tools

There are a number of helpful resources when trying to discover new educational technology tools. The following are some resources that might be helpful for librarians looking for additional technology tools. Six websites about educational technology tools are discussed, as well as ways to keep up with skills and training. Finally, groups and organizations that are helpful for networking and discussing technology tools are mentioned.

Find Your Hat for Libraries: https://agoge.uscupstate.edu/findyourhat

Find Your Hat for Libraries was created by five librarians, including myself, in South Carolina as part of the 2015 ILEAD USA SC program. It reviews 50 technology tools that fall under 10 hats (job duties), including instruction, emerging technologies, programming, management, and so on. Each tool is reviewed, along with examples of how the tool has been used in libraries. The site also shares how to get started and challenges of using the tool in libraries.

EdTech Teacher: http://edtechteacher.org/apps

EdTech Teacher was founded by a group of teachers and educators "to support educators in their quest to enrich student learning experiences through emerging technologies." Tools are viewable in two methods: tools by mobile device or tools by learning activity. There are 23 learning activity categories, such as "Record and Edit Video," "Create and Edit Images," "Create Digital

Stories," and so on. The option to look at tools based on device is also beneficial for finding the best tool for a given situation.

Free Tech 4 Teachers: http://www.freetech4teachers.com

Richard Byrne is a former high school teacher who created this website to help educators discover technology tools to use in the classroom. Richard has also written for *School Library Journal* from 2012 to 2015 under the "Cool Tools" category of articles, discussing different educational technology tools for librarians and educators. He provides practical information about how to use technology tools in the classroom.

EdTech Magazine: https://edtechmagazine.com

EdTech Magazine has two versions of the website: one geared toward higher education and one geared toward K–12. Both have a large number of articles related to technology and how it is used in the classroom and more broadly in education. This is a good resource for new trends in education technology and the reasons for using educational technology in the classroom.

EdTech Digest: https://edtechdigest.wordpress.com

EdTech Digest is similar to *EdTech Magazine* in scope. The website shares educational technology tools, interviews, and trends. The "Cool Tools" section of the site is the best place to go to discover new technology tools and ways they can be used in libraries and education. The "Trends" area can also help librarians think about reasons for using educational technology in the classroom and how the classroom might change based on new technologies.

EdSurge: https://www.edsurge.com

EdSurge is similar in scope to *EdTech Digest* and *EdTech Magazine*. It discusses how and when to use technology in higher education and K–12 institutions. Tools are less of a focus with this resource, and trends are more thoroughly examined. There are categories of articles for postsecondary learning (higher education, adult learning, and MOOCs); learning strategies (adaptive learning, blended learning, flipped classroom, etc.); and technology in school (coding, gaming, s'cool tools, etc.), among other categories.

KEEPING UP SKILLS AND TRAINING

When any new skill or ability is learned, practice makes perfect. Taking the time to play with a new technology tool makes it easier to use in the future.

Different librarians learn best in different ways, similar to students. Some librarians learn best by trying out a technology tool and thinking of ways it can be used in the library. Others may learn best by reading articles about trends in educational technology and finding tools that work well with the trends mentioned. Still others learn best through webinars or attending conferences. No matter the type of learning, it is important to realize that technology and educational technology tools change. Just as librarians are expected to learn new database layouts, librarians using educational technology tools need to learn about updates.

GROUPS AND ORGANIZATIONS

Because technology is so prevalent in libraries, there are a large number of groups and organizations that can be joined to discuss educational technology tools. One of the best organizations to join in regards to technology in education is the International Society for Technology in Education (ISTE; https://www.iste.org). The ISTE conference often overlaps in dates with the American Library Association annual conference (ALA; http://www.ala.org). This is unfortunate because many librarians will choose to participate in ALA over ISTE, even though ISTE has a stronger focus on technology. Within ALA, the following organizations are also helpful: the Library and Information Technology Association (LITA), the Association of College and Research Libraries (ACRL), and the Public Library Association (PLA). Finally, some librarians may prefer the Special Libraries Association (SLA; https://www.sla.org). All of these organizations hold a regular conference, as well as webinars that may discuss technology in libraries. Many also have LISTSERVs where technology tools are discussed.

Index

About the Author

Breanne A. Kirsch is a public services librarian and the coordinator of emerging technologies at the University of South Carolina Upstate in Spartanburg, South Carolina. She has an MLIS from Dominican University and was a 2011 American Library Association Emerging Leader and past chair of both the Imagineering Interest Group and the Game Making Interest Group with the Library and Information Technology Association. She collaborated with four other librarians in South Carolina on an ILEAD USA grant-funded project to develop the Find Your Hat website, which reviews 50 different free or low-cost technology tools and how they can be used in libraries. The librarians involved in this project led a preconference at the 2016 annual American Library Association conference, "Tech Tools and Transforming Librarianship." She also presented a workshop at the 2017 ACRL conference titled "Improve Instruction with Tech Tools: An Interactive Workshop Introducing Tools in Video Creation, Gamified Assessment, and Collaboration."